TECH TALK

Elementary Student's Book

Vicki Hollett

OXFORD
UNIVERSITY PRESS

CONTENTS

1 *Can you speak English?*

First meetings

1 (1.1) Two people meet for the first time. Listen and number the photos 1 to 4.

'I only speak a little
English.'
'Me too. Just a little, so
....¹.'

'It's ....².
....³ for
your machine.'

'Hi, I'm Eduardo Santez.'
'Hello. Nice ....
..........⁴.'

'It's ....⁵ pass.'

2 (1.1) Listen again. Write the missing words under the pictures.

3 Match a sentence (1–7) to the correct reply (a–g).

1 Welcome to São Paulo.
2 Nice to meet you.
3 What's this?
4 Is this manual in Portuguese?
5 Can you speak English?
6 Please speak slowly.
7 Thank you.

a OK, no problem.
b You're welcome.
c It's a manual for your machine.
d Thanks.
e Nice to meet you, too.
f Yes, just a little.
g No, it's in English.

4 Which words are missing in these conversations? Work with a partner. Have similar conversations.

1 A *Excuse me. Are you ...?*
  B *Yes, I ...*
  A *Hello, I'm ...*
  B *Hi, nice to ...*
  A *Nice to ..., too.*

2 A *Welcome to ...*
  B *Thanks.*
  A *Can you speak ...?*
  B *No, I'm sorry. Can you ... English?*
  A *Just a ..., so please ... slowly.*
  B *OK, no ...*

3 A *What's ...?*
  B *... manual. It's for you.*
  A *... very much.*
  B *You're ...*
  A *Is it in ...?*
  B *No, it's in English.*

Reference and telephone numbers

1 Count from 1 to 10 in English. Now count backwards: *ten, nine, …*

2 Listen and write the numbers.

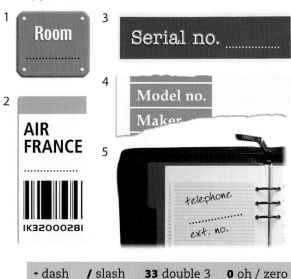

- **-** dash   **/** slash   **33** double 3   **0** oh / zero

3 Say these numbers.

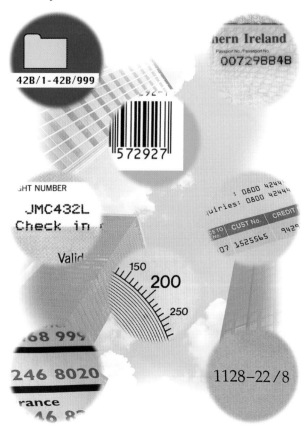

4 What parts does your telephone number have?

+44	1865	356767	ext 4260
country code	area code	number	extension

1 Write your contact numbers in the table.
2 Ask other students for their numbers and write them in the table.

What's your home telephone number?

	HOME	WORK	FAX	MOBILE PHONE*
My numbers				
Student 1:				
Student 2:				
Student 3:				

mobile phone **BrE** – cell phone **AmE**

Identifying things

1 Match the words and pictures. Write the number in the box next to the word.

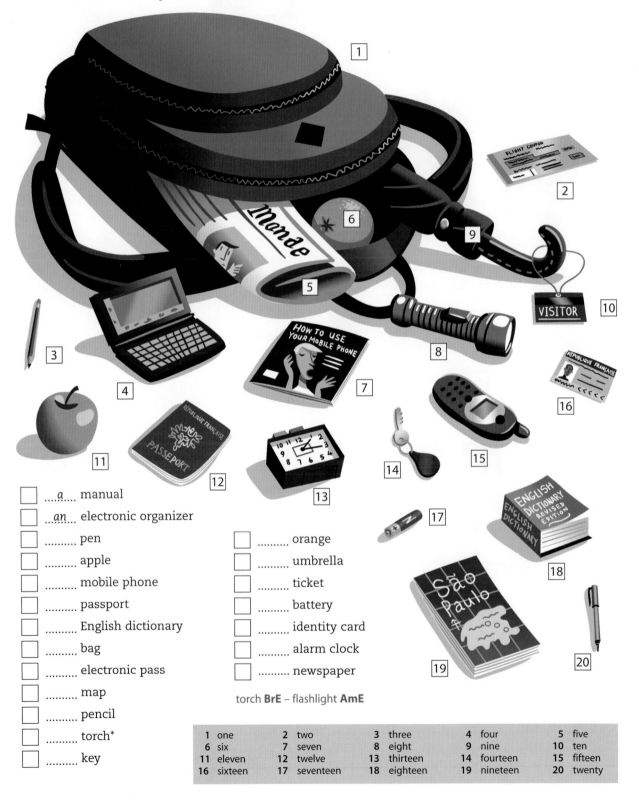

torch BrE – flashlight AmE

		...*a*... manual
		...*an*... electronic organizer
		.... pen
		.... apple
		.... mobile phone
		.... passport
		.... English dictionary
		.... bag
		.... electronic pass
		.... map
		.... pencil
		.... torch*
		.... key

		.... orange
		.... umbrella
		.... ticket
		.... battery
		.... identity card
		.... alarm clock
		.... newspaper

1 one	**2** two	**3** three	**4** four	**5** five
6 six	**7** seven	**8** eight	**9** nine	**10** ten
11 eleven	**12** twelve	**13** thirteen	**14** fourteen	**15** fifteen
16 sixteen	**17** seventeen	**18** eighteen	**19** nineteen	**20** twenty

2 (1.3) Listen and write *a* or *an* in front of the words in **1**. Look at the words. When is it *a*? When is it *an*? Complete the rules by writing *a* or *an*.

a or an?

With vowel sounds (*a*, *e*, *i*, *o*, *u*), use ....
With other sounds (*b*, *c*, *d*, *f*, etc.), use ....

3 Work with a partner. Test each other. Point to things in the picture. Ask and answer questions.

A *What's this?*
B *It's a … / an …*

4 Ask your teacher to name things in the room.

A *What's this in English?*
B *It's a chair.*

5 Test some other students.

A *What's this in English?*
B *I can't remember.*
C *It's a window.*

6 (1.4) Listen to eight sounds. Write down what each sound is, then check your answers in file 2 on page 103.

is / isn't

+ *It's an alarm clock.* (it + is = it's)
− *It isn't a siren.* (is + not = isn't)
? *Is it a keyboard?*
✔ *Yes, it is.* / ✘ *No, it isn't.*

International words

1 Complete the chart.

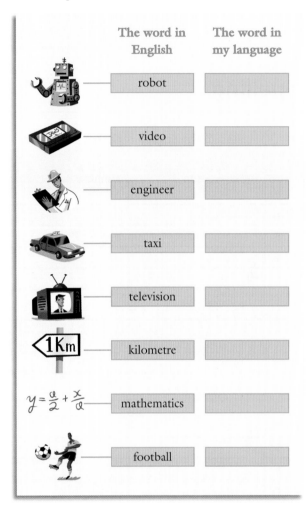

	The word in English	The word in my language
	robot	
	video	
	engineer	
	taxi	
	television	
	kilometre	
	mathematics	
	football	

2 The word *robot* is an international word. It's the same or similar in many languages. Think of more international words.

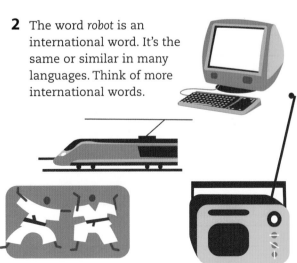

2 *How do you spell that?*

Spelling

1 (2.1) Listen to the English alphabet. Practise saying the letters.

	Pronunciation	Memory help	The NATO phonetic alphabet	My phonetic alphabet
A			Alpha	apple
B		bee	Bravo	book
C		sea	Charlie	
D			Delta	
E			Echo	
F			Foxtrot	
G			Golf	
H			Hotel	
I			India	
J		JFK	Juliet	
K			Kilo	
L			Lima	
M			Mike	
N			November	
O			Oscar	
P			Papa	
Q			Quebec	
R		are	Romeo	
S			Sierra	
T			Tango	
U		you	Uniform	
V			Victor	
W			Whisky	
X			X-ray	
Y		why?	Yankee	
Z			Zulu	

2 Say these groups of letters. Why are they in these groups?

1 B C D E G P T V   3 F L M N S X
2 A H J K   4 Q U W

3 Which letters are difficult to remember? Think of things to help you remember. Write them in 'Memory help' in the table.

4 Invent another phonetic alphabet and write it in the table.

Example
A for apple, B for book, C for coffee, D for …

5 Work with a partner. **A** – say a word. **B** – say the first letter.

A *Foxtrot.*
B *That's F.*
A *That's right.*

6 2.2 Say these company names. Then listen to eight people say who they work for. Write the number next to the correct company name.

☐ BBC   ☐ SHV   ☐ LTV
☐ SAP   ☐ GEC   ☐ NBC
☐ WSY   ☐ KAO   ☐ CSX
☐ NKK   ☐ CBS   ☐ IBM
☐ BTR   ☐ TJX   ☐ ICI

7 Work with a partner. Test each other. **A** – say a company name. **B** – point to the name.

8 2.3 A visitor spells her name. Listen and fill in line 2 of the form.

9 2.3 Listen to the receptionist again. Complete the sentences.

1 Good ....
2 .... your name, ...?
3 How .... you .... that?
4 And your .... name?
5 And .... are you with?
6 Thank you. Please .... a ....

10 Work with a partner. Act out similar conversations. Use your names and companies. Take turns to fill in lines 3 and 4 of the form in **8**.

11 Work in two teams. Play a spelling game. Team one – say an English word. Team two – spell it.

Team one *battery*
Team two *B-A-T-T-E-R-Y*

	VISITORS: 19 April			
Visitor no.	First name	Last name	Company	To see
1	Jorma	Makkinen	Lidoform	Alberto Rodriguez
2				John Heath
3				
4				
5				
6				

One to a hundred

1 Count around the class.

  1 Count from 1 to 20. *One, two, three* …

  2 Count down from 20. *Twenty, nineteen, eighteen* …

  3 Count to 100 in fives. *Five, ten, fifteen* …

  4 Count down from 100 in threes. *A hundred, ninety-seven, ninety-four* …

You can find the numbers on page 116.

2 (2.4) Listen and write the numbers.

  1 ………   4 ………   7 ………

  2 ………   5 ………

  3 ………   6 ………

3 Practise saying these numbers. Change the syllable stress.

  14 *four<u>teen</u>*   40 *<u>for</u>ty*

4 Play bingo with two or three students.

A – say the numbers in the box.

14, 45, 21, 83, 11, 76, 13, 54, 7, 16, 50, 67, 28, 98, 30, 89, 17, 48, 71, 6, 12, 38, 70, 8, 69

B – look at file 3 on page 103.
C – look at file 20 on page 107.
D – look at file 34 on page 114.

5 Complete the puzzle. Write these numbers in words.

1	10	11	12	2	20	3	13
90	4	40	5	50	16	7	8

F			S			T			N
	F		V						
	W						O		
Y									
				T		E		T	Y
E	Y								
			F						
			L						
T		R			N				

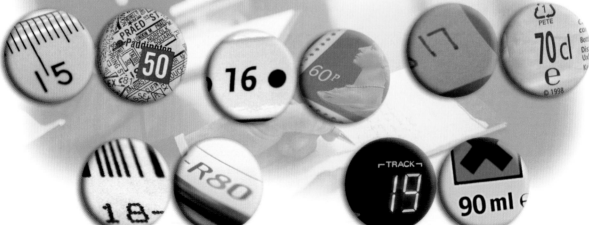

Checking an order

1 (2.5) Look at this order for some equipment. Some information on the order is wrong. Listen to a telephone call and correct the mistakes.

	Quantity	Item	Ref. / Part no.
1	16	S-hooks	IE-983
2	85	Size 12 U-bolts	MTG/62
3	72	Spring clamps	Q8236
4	40	Nylon ropes	Y-958
5	64	G-clips	WRA577
6	80	Size 18 washers	JSH 86

Sheet1

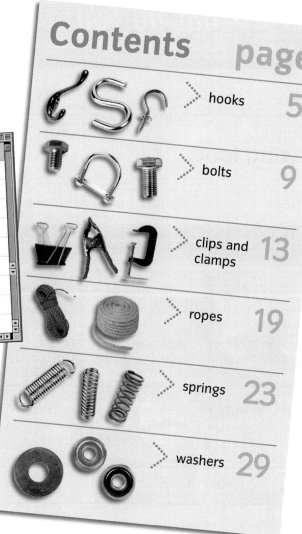

Contents page

> hooks 5

> bolts 9

> clips and clamps 13

> ropes 19

> springs 23

> washers 29

2 (2.5) Match each comment to the correct reply. Then listen again and check your answers.

1 *There are six items.*
2 Are you ready?
3 Sixteen?
4 … MTJ slash six two.
5 How many again?
6 And that's it.

a Slash six two. OK, got it.
b OK, so that's …
c *All right, what are they?*
d Yes, ready.
e That's right, sixteen.
f Fourteen.

3 Work with a partner.
  A – look at the information below.
  B – look at file 12 on page 105.

  A
This is your order. It's correct. Your partner has a copy, but it has some mistakes. Read your order so they can correct it.

QUANTITY	ITEM	REF. / PART NO.
18	S-hooks	EI-143
60	Size 10 Q-bolts	MTJ/62
12	Spring clamps	Q8236
23	Nylon ropes	Y-742
32	E-clips	WRA644
40	Size 14 washers	GSH 21

How do you spell that?

3 What do you want?

Buying food

1 Look at the menu and find the items on the order form.

2 Work with a partner. Ask and answer questions about the menu.

A *Do you want a burger?*
B *Yes, please.*
A *And what about a doughnut?*
B *No, thanks.*

3 (3.1) Listen to two people talking about the menu. Does the man want:

1 three burgers?	Yes / No
2 two cheeseburgers?	Yes / No
3 a hot dog?	Yes / No
4 fries?	Yes / No
5 a Coke?	Yes / No
6 a shake?	Yes / No
7 a doughnut?	Yes / No

4 (3.2) Listen to the order and write it on the order form in **1**. How much is the order?

5 Who says these things, the server (S) or the customer (C)? Circle S or C.

☐ That's $18.67.   S / C
☐ Yes, two cheeseburgers and one
   chicken sandwich, please.   S / C
☐ Coming right up.   S / C
☐ Yes, a medium shake.   S / C
☐ How much is it?   S / C
☐1 Can I help you?   S / C
☐ Thanks. Have a nice day.   S / C
☐ And something to drink?   S / C
☐ Great. Here you are.   S / C

6 (3.2) Put the sentences in **5** in order. Number the boxes 1 to 9. Listen again and check your answers.

7 Work with a partner. One person is the server. The other is the customer.

1 Act out a conversation. Use the words and pictures below to help you.

2 Look at the menu in **1**. Give and take more orders.

Saying what you want

1 (3.3) Listen to different people saying what they want. Number these things in the order you hear them.

.... a newspaper   .... a break
.... voicemail messages   .... a map

2 (3.3) Use words from the list to complete the sentences. Listen again and check your answers.

check	open	listen to	call	read
look at	work	write down	use	have

1 a I want to .... my office.
  b No problem. .... my phone.
  c Thank you. I just want to .... my voicemail messages.

2 a Can I .... some paper? I want to .... this address.
  b Do you want to .... a street map or metro map?

3 a Is this your newspaper?
  b Yes, do you want to .... it?
  c Yes, I want to .... the football results.

4 a Do you want to .... the window?
  b .... on a different job?

3 Work with a partner. Make up conversations with these words.

Example
A *Can I use your phone?*
B *Do you want to call the office?*
A *No, I want to order a pizza.*

1	the telephone	call the office / order a pizza
2	the manual	read the instructions / look at the diagram
3	the radio	listen to the news / check the football results
4	this pen	write down the part number / correct my spelling mistakes
5	your keys	use my car / open the office
6	the computer password	work on your emails / play a game

Specifying

1 Read the sentences about the light bulb.
Complete the sentences about the cable.

The bulb is sixty watt**s**.
It's a sixty-watt bulb.

60 W

The cable is ....·
It's a ....-.......... cable.

6 m

2 Make two sentences about these items.

Example
The battery is six volts. It's a six-volt battery.

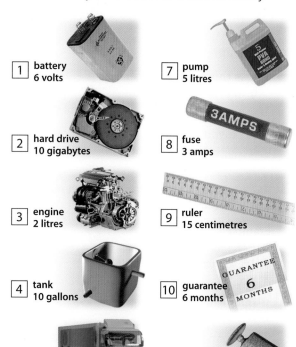

1 battery
   6 volts

7 pump
   5 litres

2 hard drive
   10 gigabytes

8 fuse
   3 amps

3 engine
   2 litres

9 ruler
   15 centimetres

4 tank
   10 gallons

10 guarantee
    6 months

5 truck
   2 tonnes

11 weight
    4 pounds

6 screw
   3 centimetres

12 ladder
    6 feet*

*Irregular plural: *one foot*, but *two **feet***.

3 Work with a partner. Make up conversations
about the items in **2**.

A *Do you want this battery?*
B *Is it six volts?*
A *Yes, it is.*
B *That's no good. I need a ten-volt battery.*
A *Oh, I see.*

A *Do you want this ...?*
B *Is it ...?*
A *Yes, it is.*
B *That's no good. I need a(n) ...*
A *Oh, I see.*

4 Complete the sentences. Write s or nothing.

Example
This ladder's six metre __s__ .
Do you have a five-metre...... cable?

1 Do you have a ten-year..... passport?
2 This bulb's 80 watt.....·
3 Is this a twenty-gigabyte..... hard drive?
4 Do we have a six-foot.... ladder?
5 The guarantee is for six month.....·
6 It's a four-hundred page.... manual.
7 Do you have twenty dollar....?
8 I need a twenty-dollar.... bill.

5 Look at this table of measurements. What do
the abbreviations mean?

Example
km = kilometre

The answers are in file 4 on page 103.

LENGTH	VOLUME	WEIGHT
1 km = 1,000 m	1 L = 1,000 ml	1 g = 1,000 mg
1 cm = 10 mm	1 gal = 8 pints	1 tonne = 1,000 kg
1 ft = 12 in		1 lb = 16 oz
1 yd = 3 ft		

6 Work with a partner. Ask and answer
questions about the table.

A *What's one kilometre?*
B *It's a thousand metres.*

7 Play a game with a partner. **A** – look at the information below. **B** – look at file 1 on page 102.

A

You and your partner both have storerooms. There are ten different items in each storeroom. The first person to find them all is the winner.

Find out what's in your partner's storeroom and write it in the correct square. Take turns to ask and answer questions like this:

A *I'll go first. What's in J16?*
B *Nothing! You missed. OK, it's my turn. What's in H18?*

My storeroom

	8	15	18	50	80
H				12 ft ladder	
I	6 m cable	7 mm screw			12 m rope
A			10 volt battery		
E	2 L pump		4 oz weight		13 amp fuse
R	2 cm bolt		100 watt bulb		

My partner's storeroom

	7	16	17	60	70
G					
B					
J					
P					
Y					

The verb *be*

+ / − / ?

The verb *be* has three forms: *am*, *are*, and *is*.
The contractions are *'m*, *'re*, and *'s*.
Use *not* to make negatives. Contraction – *n't*.
Change the word order to make questions.
You are hungry. → *Are you hungry?*

1 Write the two forms of these contractions
(*am not* has only one contraction).

1	I am not.	*I'm not.*	——
2	You are not.	*You're not.*	*You aren't.*
3	He is not.	....	....
4	She is not.	....	....
5	It is not.	....	....
6	We are not.	....	....
7	They are not.	....	....

2 Write the questions.

1	You're hungry.	*Are you hungry?*
2	He's French.	....
3	It's an electronic pass.	....
4	They're correct.	....
5	We're ready.	....
6	The numbers are wrong.	....
7	The manual's in English.	....

✓ / ✗

To answer 'yes', don't use contractions. *Yes,
she is*, not ~~*Yes, she's*~~.
To answer 'no', use contractions. *No, she isn't*.

3 Complete the answers.

1	Is she English?	*Yes, she is.*
2	Is he English?	*No, he isn't.*
3	Is it my turn?	Yes, ...
4	Are we ready?	No, ...
5	Are the cables OK?	Yes, ...
6	Is this room 962?	No, ...
7	Are you hungry?	No, ...

Classroom instructions

Complete the instructions with verbs from
the list.

Say	Spell	Listen to
Write	Check	Look at
Read	Open	Work with

1 .*Read*. the instructions.

2 .... your book.

3 .... the picture.

4 .... the cassette.

5 .... the word.

6 .... the word.

7 .... the number.

8 .... a partner.

9 .... your answers.

At reception

1 Complete the conversation with words and phrases from the list

What's your name	no problem	Sorry
what company	do you spell	to see
here you are	Thanks	room
a little English		

A Good morning.

B Good morning. I'm here ....¹ Emma Tanner.

A ....², please?

B Svenson. Ulf Svenson.

A How ....³ that?

B S-V-E-N-S-O-N.

A And ....⁴ are you with?

B Sundsvall Engineering.

A Is this your first visit?

B ....⁵?

A Is this your first visit here?

B Yes, it is. Sorry, I only speak ....⁶.

A OK, ...⁷. Do you have a passport?

B Yes, ...⁸.

A ....⁹. That's fine, Mr Svenson. Emma Tanner is in ....¹⁰ 406.

2 Read the conversation with a partner.

Parts and equipment

1 Match the words in the list to the correct picture in the grid below.

Write the square number. (You can ask your teacher for help or use a dictionary.)

screw	..E4..	socket	....
washer	....	tape measure	....
spring	....	ruler	....
clip	....	hard hat	....
hook	....	glove	....
belt	....	microphone	....
nut	....	camera	....
bolt	....	disk	....
clamp	....	bulb	....
cog	....	cart	....
gauge	....	lead	....
fuse	....	pallet	....
drill	....	bottle	....
cable	....	pipe	....
hose	....	paintbrush	....
plug	....	wheel	....

2 Work with a partner. Take turns to test each other.

Example
A *What's E4?*
B *It's a screw.*

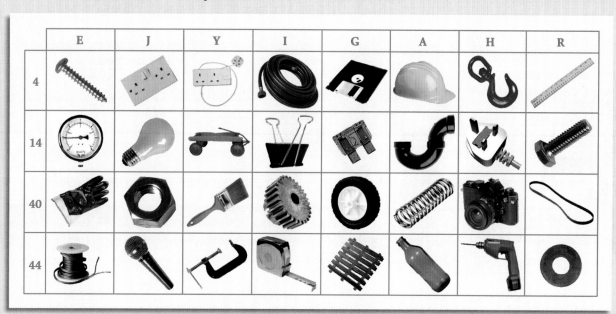

4 Is that correct?

Email addresses

1 (4.1) Listen to someone saying an email address. Tick the correct address.

1 j-luc@redtop.co.fr ☐
2 j-luc@redtop.com.fr ☐
3 j_luc@redtop.co.fr ☐
4 j_luc@redtop.com.fr ☐

Email addresses

J_Jarvie-67@topleft.com

underscore   hyphen   at   all one word   dot

We say *com* (not C-O-M), *co* (not C-O), *net* (not N-E-T), and *org* (not O-R-G).

2 Say these email addresses.

1 m.parks@callserve.com
2 kazuo@raper.net.jp
3 wills6328@yahoo.co.uk
4 user-info@tech.store.com.br
5 f_orth@t-lightwork.org.de

3 Work in groups. One person says their email address. The others write it down.

Telephone messages

1 (4.2) Listen to someone taking a telephone message. Write the message.

| Message for: | *Maria* |

Please call:

Telephone no:

2 Complete the sentences with a phrase from the list.

| I'm afraid | do you | a second | Can I |
| Can you | I need | This is | |

1 .... speak to Maria, please?
2 .... she's not here.
3 .... take a message?
4 Sure. Just ....
5 .... a pen.
6 .... Don Sinclair.
7 How .... spell that?

3 (4.2) Listen again and check your answers.

Correcting

To correct someone, stress the information that's different.

A *So that's 4989 287 9806.*
B *No, 98**2**6.*

4 Work with a partner. Take turns to be **A** and **B**.

> A *So that's 6741.*
> B *No, 674**3**.*

1 A So that's 6741.   B No, 6743.
2 A So that's 8529.   B No, 9529.
3 A So that's 3290.   B No, 3490.
4 A So that's 1168.   B No, 1164.
5 A So that's 344742. B No, 347742.
6 A So that's 652880. B No, 642880.

5 Write these phrases in the correct place in the table.

How do you spell that?
The code is …
Just a second. I need a pen.
Thanks very much.
This is Jean-Luc.
So that's …

Useful telephone phrases

Starting the call
Hello.
Is that the Research Department?
.... 1
Can I speak to …, please?

Messages
Can you take a message?
Are you ready?
.... 2

Giving numbers
My number is …
.... 3

Spelling
.... 4
J-I-M. Then new word …

Checking
Sorry?
.... 5

Ending the call
.... 6
You're welcome.
Goodbye.

6 Work with a partner. Use the words in the boxes to make another call. Take turns to be **A** and **B**.
A – write the message.
B – use your real name and telephone number.

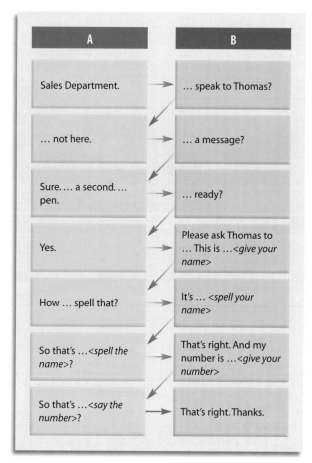

A	B
Sales Department.	… speak to Thomas?
… not here.	… a message?
Sure. … a second. … pen.	… ready?
Yes.	Please ask Thomas to … This is … *<give your name>*
How … spell that?	It's … *<spell your name>*
So that's … *<spell the name>?*	That's right. And my number is … *<give your number>*
So that's … *<say the number>?*	That's right. Thanks.

7 Work with a partner.
A – look at the information below.
B – look at file 5 on page 103.

A
You work for Allied Engineering. You work with Teresa Harris, but she isn't here today. Someone calls you. Take a message and write it here.

Message for: ....
Please contact: ....
Contact information: ....
....
....

Checking equipment

1 Read the email and look at the picture. Are all the parts correct?

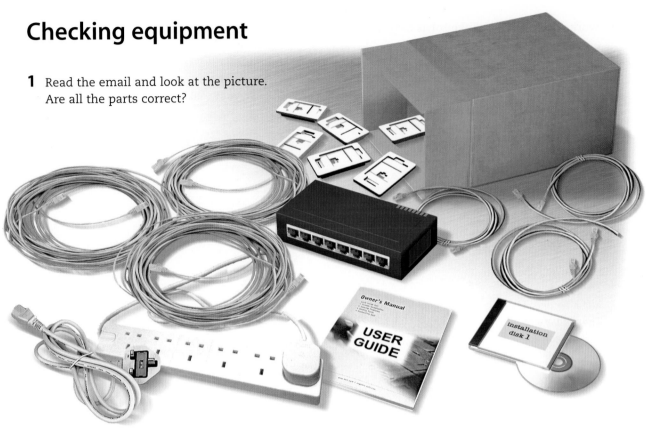

2 Work with a partner. Check the parts against the list.

A *Do we have two six-foot cables?*
B *No, we have three!*
A *Do we have ...?*

3 Marcus calls Chas, but Chas is out. Marcus leaves this message. Complete the message with the words from the list.

disk	network	six	three
need	have	call	don't

'Hi, Chas! It's Marcus. Thanks for your email about installing the ....[1]. I'm afraid we ....[2] a problem. We ....[3] have enough twenty-five-foot cables. We need four, but we only have ....[4]. We have an extra ....[5]-foot cable, but that's no good. And we have another problem. We only have one installation ....[6]. I think we ....[7] two. Please ....[8] me about this. Thanks a lot. Bye.'

4 🎧 (4.3) Listen and check your answers.

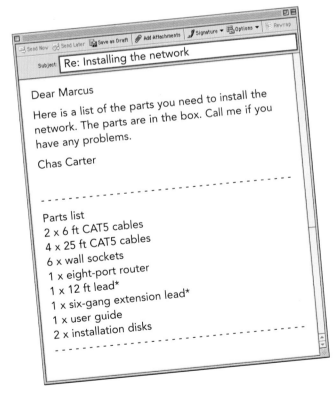

Subject: Re: Installing the network

Dear Marcus

Here is a list of the parts you need to install the network. The parts are in the box. Call me if you have any problems.

Chas Carter

- -

Parts list
2 x 6 ft CAT5 cables
4 x 25 ft CAT5 cables
6 x wall sockets
1 x eight-port router
1 x 12 ft lead*
1 x six-gang extension lead*
1 x user guide
2 x installation disks

- -

lead **BrE** – power cord **AmE**
six-gang extension lead **BrE** – six-outlet power strip **AmE**

5 Work with a partner. **A** – look at the information below. **B** – look at file 8 on page 104.

A

You need these things for a job. Ask your partner if they have them. Tick (✓) the things they have.

Do you have …?

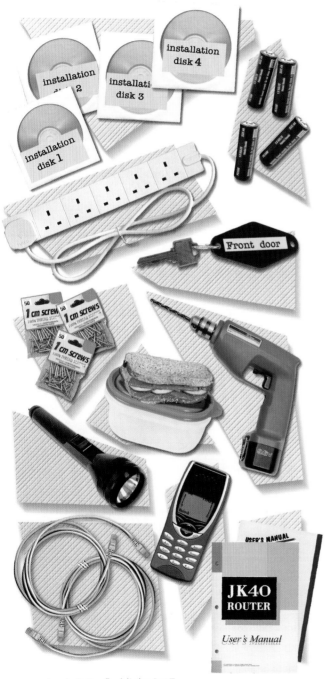

torch **BrE** – flashlight **AmE**

Following instructions

1 Look at these lines. Which is:

1 horizontal?
2 diagonal?
3 vertical?

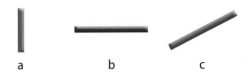

a   b   c

2 (4.4) Listen to some instructions and draw the lines on the grid. What is it?

1	2	3	4	5	6	7	8	9	10
11	12	13	14	15	16	17	18	19	20
21	22	23	24	25	26	27	28	29	30
31	32	33	34	35	36	37	38	39	40
41	42	43	44	45	46	47	48	49	50
51	52	53	54	55	56	57	58	59	60
61	62	63	64	65	66	67	68	69	70
71	72	73	74	75	76	77	78	79	80
81	82	83	84	85	86	87	88	89	90
91	92	93	94	95	96	97	98	99	100

3 Work with a partner.
A – look at the information in file 9 on page 104.
B – look at the information in file 36 on page 114.

Describing controls

1 Look at this control panel. Read the text and find these controls.

1 levers	4 clock	7 air vent
2 LCD displays	5 sockets	8 knobs
3 key pad	6 gauges	9 switches

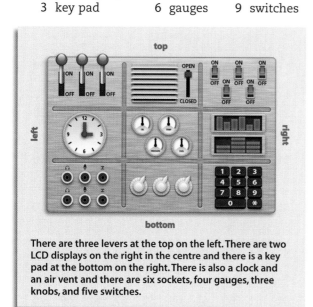

There are three levers at the top on the left. There are two LCD displays on the right in the centre and there is a key pad at the bottom on the right. There is also a clock and an air vent and there are six sockets, four gauges, three knobs, and five switches.

2 🎧 (5.1) Listen and repeat the words.

sockets   switches   knobs   gauges   levers

3 When is it *there is* ... and when is it *there are* ...? Complete the rule by choosing the right answer.

there is / there are

- For one thing, use *there is* ... / *there are* ...
- For two or more things, use *there is* ... / *there are* ...

We write *there is* ..., but we say *there's* ...

4 <u>Underline</u> the words *in*, *on*, and *at* in the text in **1**. Then complete the phrases below with *in*, *on*, or *at*.

Describing position

.... the top	.... the bottom
.... the right	.... the left
.... the centre	

5 Work with a partner. Ask and answer questions about the controls.

A *Where's the clock?*
B *It's in the centre on the left.*

A *Where are the switches?*
B *They're on the right at the top.*

6 Read about some more controls and look at the picture. There are some mistakes in the text. Find the mistakes and correct them.

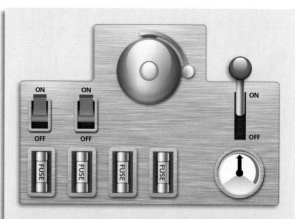

There's an alarm bell in the centre at the bottom, and there are four fuses at the bottom on the right. There are two switches at the top on the left. There's a gauge at the top on the right and a lever at the bottom. The switches are off and the lever is down.

Example
There's an alarm bell in the centre at the ~~bottom~~ *top* ...

7 Match the parts of this control station with the words in the list.

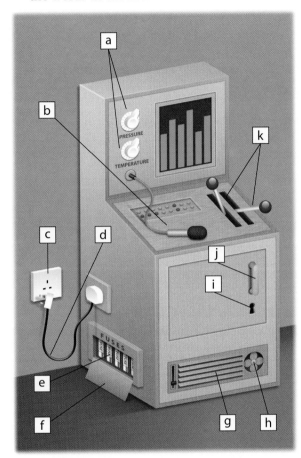

microphone	fuse	fan
handle	socket	lock
air vent	cover	lead*
levers	knobs	

lead **BrE** – power cord **AmE**

8 Look at the control station in **7** again. What do we:

1 open and close?
2 pull and push?
3 lock and unlock?
4 plug in and unplug?
5 turn clockwise and anti-clockwise*?
6 turn on and turn off?
7 remove and replace when they burn out?

anti-clockwise **BrE** – counter-clockwise **AmE**

Example
open and close – the air vent, the cover

9 Read these instructions. Point to the correct part of the control station.

1 Close the air vent.
2 Turn off the fan.
3 Pull the lever.
4 Unlock the cover.
5 Plug in the control station.
6 Turn the knobs clockwise.
7 Remove the fuse.

10 Give the opposite instructions.

Example
*Close the air vent. – **Open** the air vent.*

11 Watch your teacher mime some of the instructions. Say the instructions.

12 Work with a partner. **A** – give the instructions. **B** – mime the instructions.

13 Work with a partner. **A** – look at the information below. **B** – look at file 11 on page 105.

A
Here's another control panel. Your partner has a similar picture, but there are six differences. Describe your control panel to your partner. Find the differences.

A *There are two switches.*
B *Where are they?*
A *On the right at the top.*
B *Are they on or off?*

Describing facilities

1 Match these facilities to the correct symbol.

1 restaurant
2 stairs
3 telephones
4 car park*
5 elevator
6 toilets*
7 meeting rooms
8 coffee bar
9 photocopiers
10 Internet computers
11 smoking area
12 reception desk
13 fitness centre
14 swimming pool

car park **BrE** – parking lot **AmE**
toilets **BrE** – bathroom **AmE**

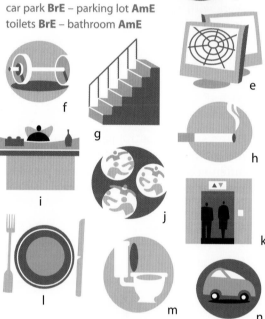

2 🎧(5.2) A hotel guest wants five things. What are they? Listen and find out.

3 What facilities are there at the hotel? Is there:

1 a restaurant in the hotel?
2 24-hour room service?
3 a restaurant near the hotel?
4 a minibar in the room?
5 an elevator?

4 🎧(5.2) Listen again and complete the questions. Then answer them.

1 ....'s the hotel restaurant?
2 .... room service?
3 .... restaurants near the hotel?
4 .... minibar in my room?
5 .... elevator?

5 When is it *Is there …* and when is it *Are there …*? Complete the rules by choosing the right answer.

Is there a(n) …? / Are there any …?

- For one thing ask *Are there any …? / Is there a(n) …?*
- For two or more things ask *Are there any …? / Is there a(n) …?*

---

6 Work with a partner. Ask and answer questions about the facilities of the building you're in now. Use the symbols in **1**.

A *Is there a restaurant?*
B *No, there isn't.*
A *Are there any stairs?*
B *Yes, there are.*

What other facilities are there?

7 Work with a partner again. Look at this elevator sign. Ask and answer questions about these facilities.

- reception desk
- coffee bar
- fitness centre
- Italian restaurant
- car park
- swimming pool
- cocktail bar
- meeting rooms

A *Where's the reception desk?*
B *It's on the first floor.*

The Prince Regent Hotel	Floor
Rooftop Pool	23
President's Fitness Club	22
Fazio's Pizzeria	12
Hawaii Nights Cocktail Bar	11
Executive Meeting Rooms	3 and 4
Rio Coffee Lounge	2
Reception	1
Parking	Lower level

Describing tests

1 Look at the pictures. How many vehicles and people are there? Are they real people?

2 Complete the conversation. Write *there's*, *there isn't*, *there are*, or *there aren't*.

Picture 1
Q How many people are there in the car?
A None, but ....¹ three dummies. ....² a dummy of a man at the front and a woman and child at the back, but ....³ any real people.
Q It's just a test?
A Yes, it's a 56 km/h crash test.

Picture 2
Q Where are the car doors?
A ....⁴ any. We want to see the dummies move.
Q What about seat belts?
A ....⁵ a seat belt at the front, and ....⁶ an air bag too. But ....⁷ a seat belt at the back.

Picture 3
Q Is this a dummy too? ....⁸ circles on its clothes.
A Yes, it's another test. ....⁹ sensors in its body too. They help us measure its movement.
Q Is there a fire here?
A No, ...¹⁰. It's an air bag.

3 Underline the plural words in the questions and answers in **2**.

Example
How many <u>people</u> are there in the car?

Plurals

1 Add -s if there is more than one thing.
   one door – two doors, one belt – three belts
2 Some plurals end with *-es* or *-ies*.
   If a word ends *-sh*, *-s*, *-ch*, *-x*, or *-z*, add *-es*.
   crashes, addresses, switches, faxes
3 If a word ends with a consonant +*-y*, remove
   -y and add *-ies*.
   dummy → dummies, battery → batteries.
4 Some plurals are irregular.
   *one person – two **people***

4 Write the plurals of these words. Add *-s*, *-es*, or *-ies*.

1 battery   *batteries*
2 sandwich   ....
3 box   ....
4 lock   ....
5 key   ....
6 security pass ....
7 dictionary   ....

5 These words have irregular plural forms. What are they? Ask your teacher for help or use a dictionary.

1 person   *people*
2 man   ....
3 woman   ....
4 child   ....
5 foot   ....
6 tooth   ....

Tell me about it

Describing features

1 What kind of car do you have (a Ford, a BMW, etc.)? Is it very old?

2 Look at the photos in **4**. What kind of car is this? Write the numbers of these parts.

1 wheels	5 windscreen*
2 steering wheel	6 brake pedal
3 seats	7 fins
4 windows	

Does it have a gear lever*?

windscreen **BrE** – windshield **AmE**
gear lever **BrE** – stick shift **AmE**

3 This Cadillac Sedan de Ville was very advanced for 1959. It has automatic transmission (not manual) and a lot of other features. Look at the features below. Which features does it have? What do you think?

Does it have:
1 *manual transmission?*   Yes / <u>No</u>
2 electrically powered windows?   Yes / No
3 a central locking system?   Yes / No
4 power brakes?   Yes / No
5 power steering?   Yes / No
6 air bags?   Yes / No
7 cruise control?   Yes / No
8 a heater?   Yes / No
9 a telephone?   Yes / No
10 a GPS (global positioning satellite) system?   Yes / No
11 air-conditioning?   Yes / No
12 a CD player?   Yes / No
13 a six-cylinder engine?   Yes / No
14 an eighty-litre fuel tank?   Yes / No
15 fins?   Yes / No
16 other features? (what?)   Yes / No

4 Read about the Sedan de Ville and check your answers.

The Sedan de Ville has all the advanced engineering features of a 1959 Cadillac. It has power brakes and electrically powered windows. Its radio has an electrically powered antenna*. An electric switch locks and unlocks all the doors from the driver's seat. Driving is easy with its automatic transmission, and it has power steering, so parking is easy too. There's a heater for cold weather and air-conditioning for hot weather. And the Sedan de Ville is powerful. It has an 8-cylinder, 390-in³ (6.4-litre) engine and a 21-gallon (80-litre) fuel tank. With the Sedan de Ville, you can save money on fuel because it has automatic cruise control.

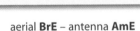

aerial **BrE** – antenna **AmE**

5 Work with a partner. Ask and answer questions about your cars. Ask about the features in **3**.

A *Does your car have automatic transmission?*
B *No, it doesn't. It's manual.*
A *Does it have …?*

have / has

+ *It has fins.*
− *It doesn't have fins.*
? *Does it have fins?*
✔ *Yes, it does.* / ✗ *No, it doesn't.*

6 Look at some more vehicles. Say what's unusual about them.

Example
Vehicle b has no pedals.

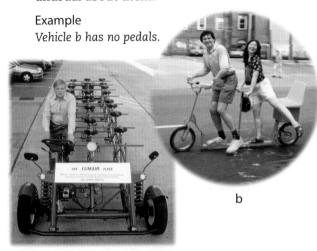

a

b

7 Which vehicle has:

1 no wheels?
2 just one wheel?
3 a lot of windows?
4 a lot of steering wheels?
5 no seats?

And which vehicles have:

6 no pedals?
7 several seats?
8 a lot of seats?
9 unusual wheels?
10 an unusual body?

Quantities
a(n) = one
several = some (more than two, but not a lot)
a lot of = many (a large number)

8 Play a game with some other students. One student chooses a vehicle. The others ask questions to find out which one. The first student can only answer *Yes*, *No*, or *I'm not sure*.

Does it have a lot of steering wheels?
No, it doesn't.
Does it have a brake?
I'm not sure.
Does it have several …?

c

d

e

f

g

h

Materials

1 Stand up and walk around the room with your teacher. Ask what things are made of.

You *What's this made of?*
Your teacher *It's made of glass.*

You *What are these made of?*
Your teacher *They're made of leather.*

2 What are these things made of?

3 Work with a partner. Point at different pictures and test each other.

A *What's this made of?*
B *It's made of plastic.*

4 Which materials:

1 are metals?
2 come from trees?
3 come from animals?
4 are synthetic (man-made, not natural)?

5 Find sixteen materials in the puzzle. Read across →, down ↓, and diagonally ↗ ↘ .

X	L	X	X	W	O	O	D	X	X	X
C	E	R	A	M	I	C	X	R	M	W
P	A	X	N	X	X	C	X	U	X	O
A	T	R	X	Y	I	X	I	B	G	O
P	H	X	D	T	L	N	R	B	O	L
E	E	X	S	B	I	O	O	E	L	S
R	R	A	X	M	O	X	N	R	D	T
X	L	X	U	G	L	A	S	S	X	E
P	O	L	Y	S	T	Y	R	E	N	E
X	A	S	I	L	V	E	R	D	X	L

Shapes

1

What shapes can you see in these pictures? Answer the questions. You can check your answers in file 7 on page 103.

1. How many cubes can you see?
2. Is the circle really circular?
3. Is the square really square?

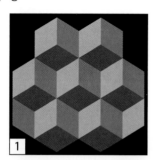

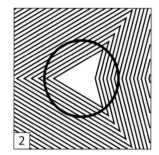

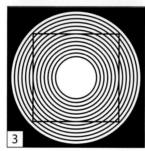

2

Complete the table using words from the list.

| semi-circle | sphere | triangular | oval |
| cylindrical | square | rectangular | cube |

The shape		The description	
	It's a circle.		It's circular. / It's round.
	It's a square.		It's ....¹.
	It's a triangle.		It's ....².
	It's a ....³.		It's semi-circular.
	It's a rectangle.		It's ....⁴.
	It's an ....⁵.		It's oval.
	It's a ....⁶.		It's spherical.
	It's a ....⁷.		It's cubic.
	It's a cylinder.		It's ....⁸.

3

Work with a partner. Ask and answer questions about these things.

What shape is the car?
It's spherical.

What shape is the watch?
It's triangular.

Review and Remember 2

The verb *have*

+ / ? / –

1 Use *have* with I, you, we, and they.
   You **have** mail.
2 Use *has* with he, she, and it.
   It **has** an attachment.
3 Use *do* or *does* to make questions.
   Do you have my email address?
   Does the email have an attachment?
4 Use *don't* or *doesn't* to make negative sentences.
   I **don't** have your email address.
   It **doesn't** have an attachment.

Complete this conversation, then read it with a partner.

A Do we ....¹ everything?
B Yes, we're ready to go.
A ....² you have the microphones?
B Yes, and I ....³ the lights and the video camera.
A ....⁴ you have the batteries for the camera?
B No, the camera ....⁵ have batteries. I think they're missing.
A ....⁶ it have a lead?
B Yes, it ....⁷ a 12-foot lead.
A That's OK, then.
B There's one thing we ....⁸ have.
A What's that?
B Lots of time. Come on. Hurry up!

have and *have got*

English speakers use *have* and *got* in different ways. For example, people say:
Do you have a problem? Yes, I do.
Have you got a problem? Yes, I have.
You gotta problem? Yeah, I do.
They mean the same thing.

First, second, third

1 Number the days of the week.

☐ Tuesday   ☐ Thursday
☐ Friday   ☐ Saturday
☐ Wednesday ☐ Sunday
[1] Monday

2 Number the months of the year.

☐ October   ☐ April
☐ July   ☐ September
[1] January ☐ March
☐ June   ☐ November
☐ February   ☐ May
☐ December   ☐ August

3 Number the seasons of the year.

☐ autumn*
☐ winter
☐ summer
☐ spring

autumn **BrE** - fall **AmE**

4 Work with a partner. Take turns testing each other.

A *What's the first day of the week?*
B *Monday. What's the eighth month of the year?*
A *August. What's the ...?*

See page 116 for a list of ordinal numbers.

Opposites

Complete the crossword puzzle. Use words with opposite meanings.

Example
1 *down – The opposite of* **goodbye** *is* **hello**.

Across		Down	
4	open	1	goodbye
6	hot	2	anti-clockwise
7	unlock	3	push
9	horizontal	5	on
11	plug in	8	up
12	difficult	10	left
14	top	13	no

What's missing?

1 What things are missing in these pictures?

2 Write sentences about what's missing. Check the list for help.

Example
2 *They don't have tails.*
10 *It doesn't have a floor 13.*

floor 13	@ symbols	taps	tails
wheels	pedals	stamp	plug
antenna	handles	key pads	lens

7 What can it do?

can and *can't*

1 Read about ASIMO. Is he a toy or is he a real robot?

Meet ASIMO
(**A**dvanced **S**tep in **I**nnovative **MO**bility)

ASIMO is a humanoid robot, developed by the Honda Motor Co. He is 120 cms tall and he weighs 43 kgs. You can control him with a computer or give him voice instructions. ASIMO is a service robot. He is designed to help people. He can walk and climb stairs, so he can carry food upstairs to a sick person and do other jobs around the home.

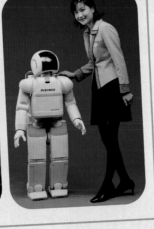

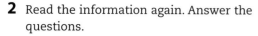

Here are ten things ASIMO can do.

1. walk forwards and backwards
2. bend and straighten his joints
3. adjust the size of the steps he takes
4. climb up and down stairs
5. turn left, right and around
6. raise and lower his arms 105 degrees
7. operate light switches
8. open and close doors
9. carry loads
10. push carts

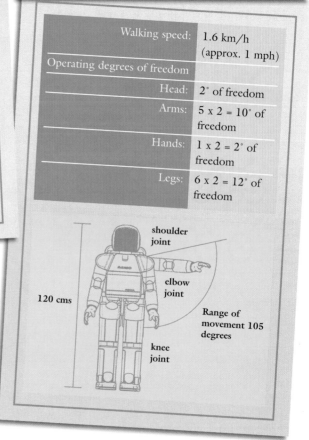

Walking speed:	1.6 km/h (approx. 1 mph)
Operating degrees of freedom	
Head:	2° of freedom
Arms:	5 x 2 = 10° of freedom
Hands:	1 x 2 = 2° of freedom
Legs:	6 x 2 = 12° of freedom

shoulder joint

elbow joint

120 cms

Range of movement 105 degrees

knee joint

2 Read the information again. Answer the questions.

1. What is ASIMO?
2. Which company developed ASIMO?
3. Can ASIMO understand voice instructions?
4. Can ASIMO turn on a light?
5. Can ASIMO take small and large steps?
6. Can ASIMO run?

3 Look at the list of ten things ASIMO can do in **1**. Match them with the correct picture.

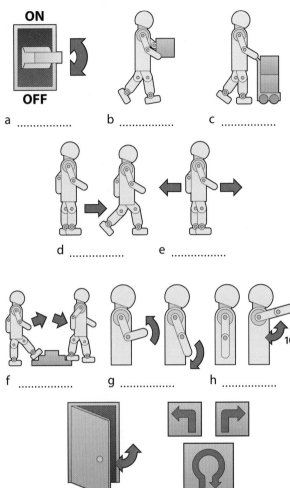

a ....   b ....   c ....

d ....   e ....

f ....   g ....   h ....

i ....   j ....

4 ASIMO can't raise his arm more than 110 degrees. And he can't dance. Think of more things he can't do. Work with some other students. Make a list.

Example
He can't swim. He can't use a telephone.

5 Imagine your teacher is ASIMO. Give them instructions for things they *can* do, for example, switch on the light, open the door, etc. Give them instructions for things they *can't* do too.

A *Walk forwards two steps. Raise your left arm. Switch on the light.*
B *I can't! I can't reach the switch!*

Body parts

1 Point to these parts of your body.

leg	foot	neck	head	mouth	nose
arm	teeth	back	hand	face	jaws

2 Match the body parts with the words in **1**.

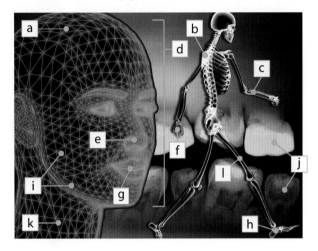

3 We use these words to describe other things. Write the names of the parts in these pictures.

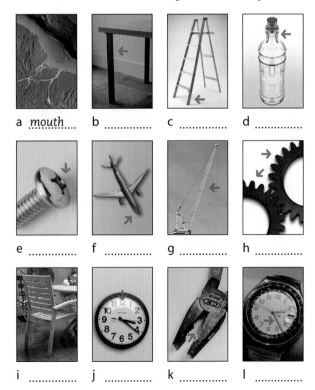

a *mouth*   b ....   c ....   d ....

e ....   f ....   g ....   h ....

i ....   j ....   k ....   l ....

Explaining what things do

1 What can these robots do? Say what you think.

☐ Robug 3

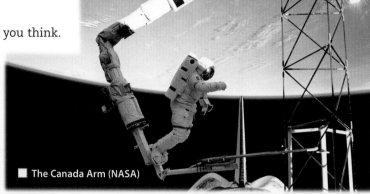
■ The Canada Arm (NASA)

☐ Sirius

☐ RL800

☐ IRB 840

☐ Sony's Robot Dog

2 (7.1) Check your answers. Listen to different people talking about the robots. Number the photos in the order you hear about them.

3 Which robot:

1 is fully automatic?
2 can reach 15 metres?
3 is an electronic pet?
4 has vacuum gripper feet?
5 is the solution for dirty windows?
6 is designed to save floor space?

4 (7.1) Listen again and write the missing numbers.

1 Robug 3 can pull loads of .... lb.
2 Sirius can clean .... m² of glass in just one hour.
3 The IRB 840 has a maximum load of .... kg.
4 The International Space Station is .... miles above the earth.
5 The RL800 is only $ ....
6 This Sony robot dog is .... mm long.

Saying hundreds

In British English, say *and* before the tens.
Two hundred and twenty-one pounds.
In American English, you can say *and* or not say *and*.
Three hundred and twenty feet or *Three hundred twenty feet*.

5 Practise saying the numbers in **4**.

Two hundred and twenty-one pounds.
A hundred and twenty square metres.

6 Work with a partner. **A** – look at the information in file 6 on page 103. **B** – look at the information in file 10 on page 105.

Dimensions

1 What kind of robot is this? What can it do? Read about the Robosaurus and find out.

The Robosaurus is a 12-metre-high entertainment robot. It's designed to lift, crush, and burn cars. It weighs 26 tonnes and it's controlled by a human pilot who sits inside its head. 60 m flames come out of its nose, and its mouth opens and closes with a pressure of 140 kg/cm². It can lift cars 15 m in the air and bite them in half with its 30 cm teeth. After shows, the robot becomes a trailer and it can travel by road to the next city. It can fold up to just 14½ metres long, 4 metres high, and 2½ metres wide.

SPECIFICATIONS

Height (standing)	*12m*
Height (folded up)	
Length (folded up)	
Width (folded up)	
Length of teeth	
Jaw pressure	
Weight	

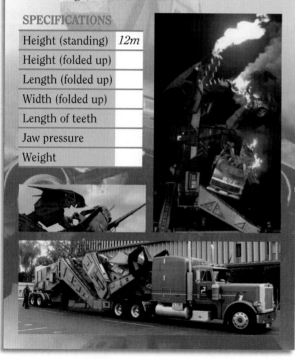

2 Complete the specifications above.

3 Work with a partner. Take turns to ask and answer these questions about Robosaurus.

1 When it's standing, how high is it?
2 When it's folded up, how high is it?
3 How long is it?
4 How wide is it?
5 How long are its teeth?
6 What's its jaw pressure?
7 How heavy is it?

4 Here are some questions about another robot. Complete the words.

1 How h.......... is it?   4 in
2 How w.......... is it?   8 in
3 How l.......... is it?   8 in
4 How h.......... is it?   275 g
5 How m.......... is it? $150

5 Work with a partner.
A – look at the information below.
B – look at the information in file 14 on page 106.

A

1 Use the specifications to answer questions about Line Tracker.
2 Ask your partner questions about Hyper Peppy and complete the table.

LINE TRACKER can follow black lines on white paper.

HYPER PEPPY can change direction when it hears a loud noise or things are in its way.

SPECIFICATIONS	
Height	97 mm
Length	157 mm
Width	143 mm
Weight without batteries	250 g
Price	$49.95

SPECIFICATIONS	
Height	
Length	
Width	
Weight without batteries	
Price	

8 What do you need?

Asking for things

1 (8.1) Listen to someone asking a computer technician for help. Complete the technician's task list.

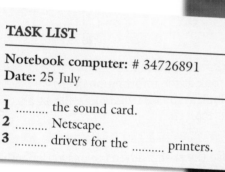

TASK LIST

Notebook computer: # 34726891
Date: 25 July

1 .... the sound card.
2 .... Netscape.
3 .... drivers for the .... printers.

2 (8.1) Listen again. Does the man need:

a   a new sound card?
b   a password?
c   a browser?
d   drivers for the network printers?
e   his computer tomorrow?

What does the technician need?

3 When is it *it* and when is it *them*?

A   *My sound card doesn't work.*
B   *OK, I'll replace* **it**.

A   *I need some drivers.*
B   *OK, I'll install* **them**.

Complete the rules by writing *them* or *it*.

> **them** and **it**
>
> .... refers back to one thing.
> .... refers back to two or more things.

4 Work with a partner. Take turns to be **A** and **B**.
A – say the problem.
B – say what you'll do.

A   *I need Internet Explorer.*
B   *I'll install it.*

A   *Are there 60 nails here?*
B   *I'll count them.*

1   *I need Internet Explorer.* (install)
2   *Are there 60 nails here?* (count)
3   There are some mistakes on this diagram. (correct)
4   The aerial is bent. (straighten)
5   The wheels are dirty. (clean)
6   The door's locked. (unlock)
7   These bags are heavy. (carry)
8   The pump doesn't work. (replace)
9   We don't need this cover. (remove)
10   We need 13-amp fuses. (order)
11   The window's open. (close)

5 Match the words to the correct picture.
Which are singular and which are plural?

1 scissors
2 hose
3 pliers
4 cart
5 scales
6 ruler
7 tape measure
8 headphones
9 wrench
10 goggles

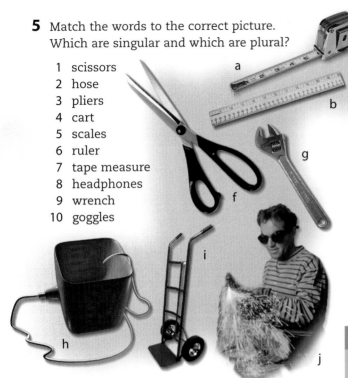

6 Work with a partner. Take turns to be **A**
and **B**. **A** – say what you need to do. **B** – ask
what **A** needs.

A *I need to cut something.*
B *Do you need some scissors?*
A *Yes. Do you have any?*

A *I need to fill the tank.*
B *Do you need a hose?*
A *Yes. Do you have one?*

1 cut something
2 fill the tank
3 protect my eyes
4 draw a straight line
5 measure the floor
6 weigh something
7 move some boxes
8 loosen a bolt
9 remove a nail
10 listen to a CD

7 Work in groups. Imagine you need these
things. Explain why you need them. Think of
lots of different reasons.

Example *a computer*

A *I need to access the Internet.*
B *I need to write a letter.*
C *I need to …*

– a computer
– a password
– a mobile phone
– an English dictionary
– more money
– more time

Decimal numbers

1 (8.2) Listen to these numbers. Write the
missing words.

1 3.46   three point .... six
2 23.4   .... three point four
3 0.8   .... point eight
4 1.06   one point .... six

Decimals

- Write decimal points as a point (.), not a
comma (,).
3.5   ~~3,5~~
- After the point say numbers separately.
1.25 *one point two five*
- Before the point say numbers together.
25.25 *twenty-five point two five*
- Before the point 0 is *zero* or *nought* (not *oh*).
0.3 *zero point three* or *nought point three*
~~oh point three~~
- After the point, 0 is *zero* or *oh*.
0.03 *zero point zero three* or *zero point oh three*

2 Practise saying these numbers.

13.4   13.13   0.6   8.304   0.709

3 (8.3) Listen to three people changing money.
Write the exchange rate.

1   dollars ....

2   pesos ....

3   yen ....

4 Work with a partner.
A – look at file 16 on page 106.
B – look at file 13 on page 105.

Getting information

1 Match each sentence to the correct picture.

a ......

b ......

c ......

d ......

1 It can travel forwards, but it can't travel backwards.

2 It can travel forwards and backwards, but it can't turn left or right.

3 It can turn left or right, but it can't move up or down.

4 It can move in any direction if the wind is in the right direction.

2 The Skylark is a helicopter you can build yourself. Read the answers to some FAQs (Frequently Asked Questions). The questions are missing. Think of possible questions for the answers.

SKYLARK FAQs ● ● ●

1 Q *Can it really fly?*
A Yes it can. It can do vertical take-offs and landings and it can fly forwards, backwards, left, and right.

2 Q ....?
A 17 ft.

3 Q ....?
A 7 ft.

4 Q ....?
A Aluminium and steel.

5 Q ....?
A 350 lbs when it's empty.

6 Q ....?
A Its top speed is 95 mph.

7 Q ....?
A Just one.

8 Q ....?
A Yes, you can.

9 Q ....?
A The full-size plans are just $175.

10 Q ....?
A Visit our website at www... .

3 Here are the questions. Match them to the correct answers. Take turns asking and answering the questions with a partner.

a How fast is it?
b How long is it?
c What's it made of?
d *Can it really fly?*
e How much is it?
f How many seats are there?
g How can I get more information?
h How heavy is it?
i How high is it?
j Can I really build a Skylark myself?

Tools and equipment

1 What different things do these people need?

2 Which people need the items in this list?

a screwdriver	a plug	a funnel
a new tyre	a hammer	a saw
a plaster	a map	a paintbrush
a spirit level		

3 When is it *need* and when is it *needs*? Choose the correct answer.

1 I *need / needs* some help.
2 You *need / needs* a hammer.
3 He *need / needs* a paintbrush.
4 She *need / needs* a saw.
5 It *need / needs* a plug.
6 We *need / needs* a funnel.
7 They *need / needs* a map.

4 Work with a partner. Take turns to test each other.
A – point to a picture.
B – make a sentence.

He needs a …   She needs a …   They need a …

9 Watch out!

Warning signs

1 Match the instructions with the warning signs.

1 Don't enter. ......
2 Be careful! Don't trip. ......
3 Wear a hard hat. ......
4 Wash your hands. ......
5 Don't touch. ......
6 Wear ear protection. ......
7 Don't bring cameras in here. ......
8 Keep the aisle clear. ......
9 Use the machine's safety guard. ......
10 Open the door with care. ......
11 Keep cylinders secure and upright. ......
12 Secure your hair. ......
13 Don't bring food or drink in here. ......
14 Be careful! Slippery floor. ......
15 Lift with care. ......

2 Some signs have no instructions. Write the instructions for them.

Example
Sign v – Don't smoke.

3 Work with a partner. Test each other. One person points at a sign. The other person gives the instruction.

4 Work in groups. What warning signs do you need in your workplace? Make a list.

Example
Don't remove the safety guard.
Wear safety boots.

Colours

1 What colours are the wires?

2 (9.1) Some connections are wrong. Which wires are connected to the wrong terminals? Listen and find out.

3 (9.1) Listen again and correct the bad connections. Find the correct terminals on the picture.

should

We use *should* to say what's right or correct.
It **should** be connected to terminal B.
(Perhaps it is connected to terminal B, perhaps it isn't, but terminal B is correct.)

4 Look at the picture and say what's wrong.

Example
The black wire should be connected to terminal D.

5 Work with a partner.

A – look at the information below.
B – look at the information in file 23 on page 108.

A

1 Tell your partner how these wires should be connected.

Example
The green and white wire should be connected to terminal E.

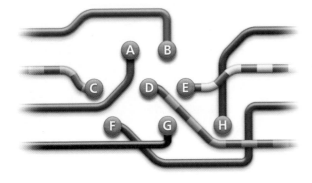

2 Listen to your partner and connect these wires.

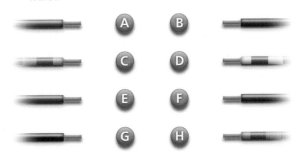

Identifying people

1 What's your job? Who do you work for?

Jobs and companies

*I'm **a** technician and he's*
__an__ engineer. .... (a or an + job)
*We work **for** BMW.* .... (for + company)

Write *a, an,* or *for* in the spaces.

1 She's .... software engineer.
2 Are you .... electrician?
3 She works .... IBM.
4 He's .... quality technician.
5 They work .... the Exxon Mobil Corporation.
6 I'm .... architect.

2 (9.2) Listen and read the comic strip. What's the story about?

3 (9.2) Listen again and write the missing words.

4 Work with a partner. Take turns to ask and answer these questions.

A *Does the security guard know Pablo?*
B *No, he doesn't.*
A *Is Pablo a service engineer?*
B *Yes, he is.*

1 *Does the security guard know Pablo?*
2 *Is Pablo a service engineer?*
3 Does Pablo work for Allied Engineering?
4 Does Pablo have a security pass?
5 Is the door open?
6 Does Pablo open the door?
7 Is the woman Pablo's customer?
8 Does she know the man with the cart?
9 Is the man a thief?

Excuse me. Yes? ___ you work here?

No, I'm ___ service engineer. I work ___ Allied Engineering and we ___ this machine. Do you have a ___ ?

Yes, it's here. Can I see it?

Ten minutes later... Er, ___ . Yes?

Can you help me? Sure, what is it?

I don't have my security pass and I want to take these computers ___ . Can you open the door ___ ___ ? How ___ I do that?

5 Work with a partner. Take turns to be Pablo and read the story.

6 Here are two rules for making questions. When do we use rule 1 and when do we use rule 2? Write 1 or 2 in the correct space.

> **Making questions**
>
> 1 Use *Do* or *Does*.
>
>   *You work here.* → *Do you work here?*
>   *He works here.* → *Does he work here?*
>
> 2 Change words around.
>   *You're an engineer.* → *Are you an engineer?*
>   *He's a thief.* → *Is he a thief?*
>
> Use rule .... with the verb *be*.
> Use rule .... with other verbs.

7 Choose the correct word to make these questions.

1 *Are / Do* you a security guard?
2 *Is / Does* your company have security guards?
3 *Are / Do* there security cameras at your company?
4 *Are / Do* visitors need security passes?
5 *Are / Do* you need a security pass?
6 *Is / Do* security a problem for your company?
7 *Is / Does* your company have security checks?

8 Work in groups. Discuss security in your companies. Ask and answer the questions in **7**. Can you do more to stop thieves?

Present Simple

+ / −

Add *s* to the verb with *he*, *she*, and *it*.
Use *don't* or *doesn't* to make negatives.

I You We They	*need more time.* *don't need more time.*
He She It	*needs more time.* *doesn't need more time.*

1 Write *s* or nothing in the spaces.

I work...... for IBM. He work s.... for Siemens.

1 This switch operate..... the lights.
2 You need..... more time.
3 We fill..... the tank with oil.
4 My wife speak..... English.
5 The joints bend..... and straighten.......

2 Write the negative forms of these sentences.

1 I know.   *I don't know*.....
2 We understand.   ....
3 He wants his money.   ....
4 The pump works.   ....
5 The wheels turn round.   ....

? / ✔ / ✗

Use *do* or *does* to make and answer questions.

Do *you need more time?*
Yes, we **do***. / No, we* **don't***.*

Does *she need more time?*
Yes, she **does***. / No, she* **doesn't***.*

3 Complete this form. Choose *do* or *does*.

■ COMPUTER USE ■

1 Do/Does you have a computer at home?	**Yes/No**
2 Do/Does your home computer have Internet access?	**Yes/No**
3 Do/Does you use a computer at work?	**Yes/No**
4 Do/Does it have Internet access?	**Yes/No**
5 Do/Does it need more memory?	**Yes/No**
6 Do/Does you play games on it?	**Yes/No**

4 Work with a partner. Take turns to ask and answer the questions.

Example
A *Do you have computer at home?*
B *Yes, I do. / No, I don't.*

What can you do?

What can you do in English? Can you:

1 name these colours?

2 say the letters of the English alphabet?
3 spell your company's name?
4 say your email address?
5 say the days of the week?
6 say the months of the year?
7 tell the time?
8 say these decimal numbers?
    5.6   2.98   29.15   0.7   4.03

What's wrong?

1 What's wrong with these instructions?

 a **Turn left.**

 b **Push the handle.**

 c **Draw a vertical line.**

 d **Turn right.**

 e **Wear gloves.**

 f **Connect the green wire to the yellow wire.**

 g **Straighten the pipe.**

 h **Go downstairs.**

2 Correct the mistakes. Write the correct instructions.

Example   *Turn ~~left~~ right.*

3 Work with a partner.
A – Read an instruction.
B – Say what it should be.

Example   A *Turn left.*
          B *It should be 'turn right'.*

Opposites

1 Write the adjectives in the list under the correct picture.

late	wrong	cold	new	clear	loose
dirty	unplugged	empty	quiet	young	expensive
heavy	small	wet	slow	deep	off

1 big / large ≠

....

2 light ≠

....

3 noisy ≠

....

4 shallow ≠

....

5 inexpensive / cheap ≠

....

6 on ≠

....

7 full ≠

....

8 connected / plugged in ≠

....

9 clean ≠

....

10 old ≠

....

11 old ≠

....

12 tight ≠

....

13 fast ≠

....

14 hot ≠

....

15 correct ≠

....

16 early ≠

....

17 dry ≠

....

18 blocked ≠

....

2 Work with a partner. Point to the pictures and ask and answer questions.

A *Is it heavy?*   B *No, it's light.*

3 Think of things to describe with the adjectives.

My dictionary is new.   Our teacher's car is dirty.

10 *Here or there?*

Locating things

1  What's lost? Where is it?
Listen and find out.

2 Answer the questions.

1 Why is he in a hurry?
2 Where's the meeting?
3 Where are his car keys?
4 What's the time?

3 Listen again and complete the sentences.

1 It's not .... the door with the other
manuals?
2 Is it .... a file?
3 Is it .... the shelf .... the boxes?
4 No, I think it's .... a bag.
5 What's that .... the radiator?
6 Look, they're .... the papers ....
.... the monitor.

4 Look at the picture of the office and
complete the sentences. Use the words in
the list.

on	under	in front of	between
in	next to	behind	

1 The scissors are .... the desk drawer.
2 The manuals are .... the door.
3 The papers are .... the monitor.
4 The disks are .... the desk.
5 The telephone book is .... the boxes.
6 The glasses are .... the keyboard.
7 The gloves are .... the desk.

5 Work with a partner.
A – you need the things in list A.
B – you need the things in list B. Look at the picture. Have conversations like this:

A *Can you see my manual?*
B *Is it behind the door?*
A *No, it isn't.*
B *Is it in the green bag?*
A *Yes, it is! Thank you!*

B *Can you see my keys?*
A *Are they on the shelf?*
B *No, they aren't.*
A *Are they in front of the monitor?*
B *Yes, they are. Thanks!*

List A	List B
newspaper	keys
manual	electric drill
batteries	watch
gloves	wallet
passport	computer disks
tape measure	telephone book
reading glasses	photos
dictionary	calculator
tool box	umbrella
scissors	mobile phone
coffee	sandwiches

6 Play a game with a coin. Your teacher leaves the room and you hide the coin. When they come back, answer their questions.

Example
Your teacher *Is it near the window?*
You   *Yes, it is.*
Your teacher *Is it under the table?*
You   *No, it isn't.*
Your teacher *Is it …?*

When your teacher finds the coin, another person leaves the room. Hide the coin again and continue the game.

Telling the time

1 Look at your watch. What's the time?

Saying times

We can say times in different ways.

1
seven o'clock
seven

2
seven fifteen
quarter past seven

3
three thirty
half past three

4
eight forty-five
quarter to nine*

5
six ten
ten past six

6
eleven fifty-five
five to twelve*

AmE – *quarter to nine* or *quarter of nine*; *five to twelve* or *five of twelve*; *ten past six* or *ten after six*.

2 Work with a partner. Take turns to ask and answer questions about these times.

A *What time is it?*
B *It's nine thirty.*

3 What time do you:

get up in the morning?
start work?
finish work?
go to bed at night?

this and *that*

1 (10.2) Listen to the conversations. Complete the sentences.

1

A Can you help me?
B Sure, what's the problem?
A It's .... bulb. It's burnt out.
B There's a new bulb in .... box over there.

2

A Are you busy?
B No, what's up?
A It's .... batteries. They're flat.
B There are some new batteries in .... boxes over there.

2 Look at the pictures again.

Picture 1 Is the bulb near the people? What about the box?
Picture 2 How many batteries and boxes are there? Are they near the people?

Complete the rules by writing *this*, *that*, *these*, or *those*.

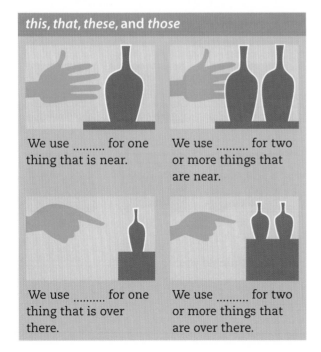

this, *that*, *these*, and *those*

We use .... for one thing that is near.

We use .... for two or more things that are near.

We use .... for one thing that is over there.

We use .... for two or more things that are over there.

3 What colours are these keys and doors? Which keys unlock which doors? Look at the pictures and complete the table.

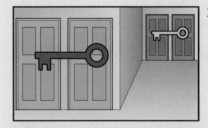

1 This key unlocks that door.

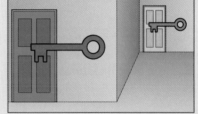

2 This key unlocks these doors.

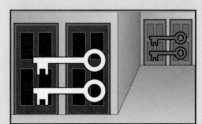

3 Those keys unlock those doors.

4 Look at the picture. What colour are:

1 the trucks?
2 the cables?
3 the rolls of tape?

5 Read the instructions and answer the questions.

'Put these cables in those boxes. Seal the boxes with this tape and put them on that truck. Put those cables in these boxes. Then seal the boxes with that tape and put them on this truck.'

1 Where are the green cables now?
2 Where are the yellow cables now?
3 What colour tape is on the boxes in front of the red truck?

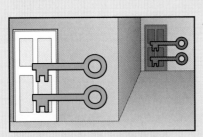

4 Those keys unlock this door.

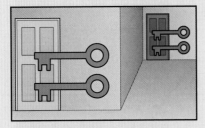

5 These keys unlock that door.

6 That key unlocks these doors.

	Key colour	Door colour
1	red	yellow
2		
3		
4		
5		
6		

What's the problem?

Suggesting solutions

1 (11.1) What's wrong with this drill? Listen and find out.

2 Why can't he:

1 use the drill?
2 plug it in at the wall?
3 use the socket over there?
4 use the extension lead?
5 buy another extension lead?

3 Work with a partner. Read the conversation together. What are the missing words?

A This [1] is no good.

B What's [2] with it?

A The [3] is flat.

B Why don't you [4] it in at the [5] ?

A I can't. There's no [6] here.

B There's a [7] .

A Yes, but it's [8] .

B Then use the [9] .

A I can't. It's [10] .

B Then [11] another one.

A That's [12] . Just [13] problem. Do you have any [14] ?

4 Look at the pictures and find something:

1 heavy 3 dangerous 5 expensive
2 hot   4 long   6 small

danger

weight
2 tonnes

a Bring me that box.

b Increase the pressure.

$250,000.

c Why don't you buy this car?

Terms & Conditions

d Read what it says.

e Hurry up and drink your coffee.

Password PP32-946011-444/PE7KY916ZAXA_00XR/2617

f Remember this password.

5 Work with a partner and explain the problems. Use *too*.

A *Bring me that box.*
B *I can't. It's too heavy.*

6 Match these problems to the best solution.

Problems
1 I'm feeling sleepy.
2 These batteries are flat*.
3 I have a headache.
4 I have no money.
5 My watch is broken.
6 I can't reach the top shelf.
7 This rope is too long.
8 I can't remember this password.
9 This tank is empty.
10 I can't remove this cover.

Solutions
a Take an aspirin.
b Write it down.
c Buy a new one.
d Hit it with a hammer.
e Have some strong coffee.
f Cut it in half.
g Find a cash machine.
h Fill it.
i Use a ladder.
j Replace them.

flat batteries **BrE** – dead batteries **AmE**

7 Work with a partner.
A – read a problem.
B – suggest a solution. Say *Why don't you …?*

Example
A *I'm feeling sleepy.*
B *Why don't you have some strong coffee?*
A *That's a good idea. / OK, I will.*

8 Match the problems with the correct picture.

1 I can't remember English words.
2 I want to lose weight.
3 My computer is very slow.
4 I want to reduce my electricity bills.

a

b

c

d

9 Work with some other students. One person explains a problem. The others suggest different solutions. Try to suggest a lot of solutions.

Impossible and necessary

1 (11.2) Is parking a problem in your city? Look at the picture. What's the problem? Listen and find out.

2 Complete the conversation.

A Sorry, you ....¹ park here. You ....² move.
B Where can we park?
A There's a car park* down the street.
B But it's full.
A Then you ....³ use a meter.
B But we ....⁴ find a meter.
A Sorry, but that sign means no parking.

car park **BrE** – parking lot **AmE**

3 Which phrase means 'it's necessary'? Which phrase means 'it's impossible'? Complete the rules with *can't* and *have to*.

can't and **have to**
Use .... if something is necessary.
Use .... if something is impossible.

4 Complete the information about these UK parking signs. Use *can't* or *have to*.

1 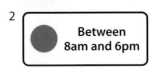 This sign means you .... park at any time. You .... find another place to leave your car.

2 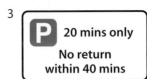 This sign means you can park, but it's restricted. You .... read the times on the sign. You .... park on this street between 8 a.m. and 6 p.m.

3 This sign also means parking is restricted. You can park on this street for 20 minutes, but then you .... move your car. You .... come back and park again for 40 minutes.

5 What do these signs mean? Work with a partner. Take turns to ask and answer questions. Use the words under the signs.

A *What does this sign mean?*
B *It means you can't / have to …*

1 turn right.

2 stop.

3 overtake.

4 make a U-turn.

5 turn left.

6 slow down.

7 drive over 30 mph.

8 watch out for children.

6 Read about driving and traffic in Mexico City and Bangkok.

What are the things José and Sanghop:
1 can't do?
2 have to do?

José

'I have to leave my car at home on Wednesdays because of the air pollution. The government restricts the number of cars in Mexico City. The last number of my licence plate is three. On Wednesdays 'threes' and 'fours' can't drive. And on Thursdays 'ones' and 'twos' can't drive, and so on. So on Wednesdays, I have to get a ride with a friend or take a bus.'

Sanghop

'The traffic in Bangkok is terrible. Some evenings I can't get home. I have to stay with a friend and sleep on their floor. We have a lot of tuk-tuks. They are open taxis for one or two people. There are no sides and the air is very dirty. I have to take my clothes to the cleaner's after the ride.'

7 Is the traffic bad in your city? Do you know other places with bad traffic problems? What happens in other cities?

8 Work with some other students. Imagine a foreign visitor is coming to your city. They want to know about driving and traffic. Think of things drivers:

1 can't do
2 have to do.

Make lists. Here are some ideas to help you start.

speed restrictions
age restrictions
tests
documentation (driving licence? insurance?)
mobile phones
seat belts

Example

You can't drive over 90 km/h on motorways in Norway. That's 56 mph. You have to wear seat belts at all times, and you have to …

12 What's going on?

Work tasks

1 Look at the pictures.

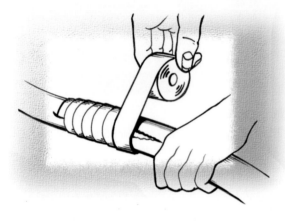

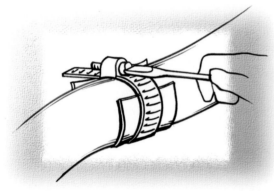

1 What are these people doing?
2 What are they using?
3 Which repair is better? Why?

2 🎧 Listen to two people talking about a repair.

1 What's the woman doing?
2 Why?
3 Is she replacing it?
4 Is she using tape?
5 What's the problem with tape?

3 🎧 Which words from the conversation are missing? Can you remember? Write them down. Then listen again and check your answers.

A What ....¹ doing?
B ....² fixing this hose.
A Why?
B Because ....³ leaking.
A Are you ....⁴ it?
B No, I'm ....⁵ it. It's a very small leak.
A Are you ....⁶ tape?
B No, ...⁷ .
A Because tape's no good.
B I know.
A Tape doesn't last.
B I know. ....⁸ using tape. I'm using a clamp.
A Clamps are better.
B I know. That's why ....⁹ a clamp.
A OK!

4 Work with a partner. Take turns to be **A** and **B** and read the conversation.

Present Continuous

To say what's happening now, use the verb *be* and *-ing*.
I'm fixing this hose. It's *leaking*.
Change the word order for questions.
You are replacing it. → *Are you replacing it?*
Use *not* for negatives.
I'm not using tape.

5 Complete another conversation. Use words and phrases from the list.

Why don't you	are you doing	clip
wrong with it	don't last	flat
Are you using	better	
Put that back	Hit it	

A Is that your camera?
B Yes, it is.
A What's <u>wrong with it</u> ¹?
B The batteries are .... ². I'm replacing them.
A .... ³ zinc carbon batteries?
B Yes, I am.
A Alkaline batteries are .... ⁴.
B I know.
A Zinc carbon batteries .... ⁵. I have alkaline batteries in my camera.
B Great.
A .... ⁶ buy some alkaline batteries?
B Because I'm late.
A You have to close the cover.
B I'm trying but I can't. I think the .... ⁷ is broken.
A .... ⁸ with a hammer.
B I have a better idea.
A Hey, what .... ⁹?
B I'm taking your camera. Thanks.
A .... ¹⁰!
B Bye!

6 Work with a partner. Take turns to be **A** and **B**. Read the conversation in **5**.

7 Tape, clamps, and clips *fasten* things and *hold* things *together*. Here are some more things that fasten and hold things together. Match the words to the correct picture.

☐ staple   ☐ hinge   ☐ cement
☐ screw   ☐ pin   ☐ button
☐ zip   ☐ bracket   ☐ paste
☐ nail   ☐ solder   ☐ padlock
☐ bolt   ☐ glue   ☐ string
☐ chain

8 What can these things fasten or hold together? Think of different materials.

Example
staple: cardboard and wood, pieces of paper

9 Watch your teacher mime using some of these things. Ask what they're doing.

Are you nailing something?
Are you pasting wallpaper?

10 Work with another student.
A – mime a verb. **B** – ask what **A** is doing.

11 Work in small groups. Watch each other doing different jobs. Say what you're doing.

A – look at file 19 on page 107.
B – look at file 21 on page 108.
C – look at file 29 on page 111.
D – look at file 35 on page 114.

some and *any*

1 (12.2) Listen to the conversation.

  1 What's the woman looking for? Does she find it?
  2 Make a list of the things she finds.

Uncountable nouns

There are two types of noun in English.

Countable nouns: *one key* *two keys*

Uncountable nouns: *chewing gum*

money

We can't count uncountable nouns, and they can't be plural.

~~one chewing gum~~ ~~two chewing gums~~ ~~one money~~
~~two moneys~~

2 (12.2) Listen again. Complete these phrases with words from the list.

keys	batteries	chewing gum
ruler	money	tape measure

  1 There's a ....
  2 There's isn't a ....
  3 There's some ....
  4 There isn't any ....
  5 There are some ....
  6 There aren't any ....

Which phrases do we use with:
• uncountable nouns?
• countable nouns?

Singulars, plurals, and uncountables

There's a(n) …
There's isn't a(n) … + singular countable noun
Is there a(n) …?   (tape measure, ruler)

There's some …
There isn't any … + uncountable noun
Is there any …?   (money, chewing gum)

There are some …
There aren't any … + plural countable noun
Are there any …?   (batteries, keys)

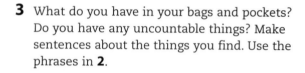

3 What do you have in your bags and pockets? Do you have any uncountable things? Make sentences about the things you find. Use the phrases in **2**.

4 Look at this storeroom. Find the things that are uncountable.

5 Work with a partner. Take turns to ask and answer questions about the storeroom. Use these phrases and the words in the list.

A *Is there a(n) …?*
B *Yes, there is. / No, there isn't.*
A *Is there any …?*
B *Yes, there is. / No, there isn't.*
A *Are there any …?*
B *Yes, there are. / No, there aren't.*

rack	table	cement	sand
windows	pipes	cart	rope
paintbrushes	string	chairs	fan
rollers	ladder	wood	petrol*
computer	lights	paper	tape
brush cleaner	paste	pallets	paint

petrol **BrE** – gasoline **AmE**

Example
A *Is there a rack?*
B *Yes, there is.*

Identifying uncountable nouns

Things that can change shape are often uncountable nouns, for example, liquids, gases, and powders.

some water   *some oxygen*   *some cement*

Some nouns can be countable or uncountable.

a rope   *some rope*
(countable)   (uncountable)

Good dictionaries say if a noun is countable [C] or uncountable [U].

6 Play a game with a partner.
   A – look at the information below.
   B – look at the information in file 18 on page 107.

A
Here is your picture. **B** has a similar picture, but there are twelve differences.
Describe your picture to **B** and find the differences.

Present Continuous

+ / –

Use the verb *be* and *-ing*.

I'm (I am) You're (You are) He's (He is) She's (She is) It's (It is) We're (We are) They're (They are)	working. not working.

? / ✔ / ✗

Change the word order to make questions.
Use the verb *be* to answer questions.

Are you listening?   Yes, we are. / No, I'm not.
Is it leaking?   Yes, it is. / No, it isn't.

1 Complete the email. Use the Present Continuous form of the verb in brackets.

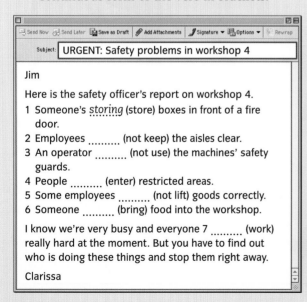

Send Now   Send Later   Save as Draft   🖉 Add Attachments   Signature ▾   Options ▾   Rewrap

Subject: URGENT: Safety problems in workshop 4

Jim

Here is the safety officer's report on workshop 4.

1 Someone's <u>storing</u> (store) boxes in front of a fire door.
2 Employees .... (not keep) the aisles clear.
3 An operator .... (not use) the machines' safety guards.
4 People .... (enter) restricted areas.
5 Some employees .... (not lift) goods correctly.
6 Someone .... (bring) food into the workshop.

I know we're very busy and everyone 7 .... (work) really hard at the moment. But you have to find out who is doing these things and stop them right away.

Clarissa

2 What questions should Jim ask the employees in workshop 4?

Are you storing boxes in front of the fire door?
Are you keeping the aisles clear?

3 What are these people doing wrong?

a   b

c   d

4 Match these warnings and instructions to the correct picture.

You can't smoke here. <u>b</u>

1 You can't put another plug in there.   ......
2 You have to use the steps.   ......
3 You have to go outside to smoke.   ......
4 Look where you're going!   ......
5 You have to find another socket.   ......
6 You can't carry all that.   ......
7 Watch out! It's falling.   ......

a, an, some, or any

1 Are these nouns countable [C] or uncountable [U]?

1	chewing gum	5	petrol	9	help
2	cart	6	password	10	money
3	water	7	glue	11	brush
4	manual	8	cable	12	paint

2 Complete the sentences with *a*, *an*, *some*, or *any*.

1 There's .... water on the floor.
2 Are there .... carts in the storeroom?
3 There's .... manual on the shelf.
4 Do you have .... extension lead?
5 There isn't .... petrol in the tank.
6 Do you need .... password for this computer?
7 I have .... glue, if you need it.
8 We don't have .... scissors.
9 There's .... stapler in my desk drawer.
10 Are you .... engineer?
11 I need .... help.
12 Do you have .... money?

Prepositions

Label the diagrams with the correct prepositions.

in front of	under	on
between	behind	
next to	in	

1 ....

2 .... 3 .... 4 ....

5 .... 6 .... 7 ....

Fastening things

1 Match the verbs in the list to the correct picture.

bolt	......	screw	......
button	......	solder	......
chain	......	spread	......
lay	......	staple	......
nail	......	stick	......
padlock	......	tie up	..1..
pin	......	zip up	......

2 Complete the instructions with a verb from the list in **1**.

1 *Tie up* ...... the box with string and .... a label on it.
2 .... your boots and .... your coat.
3 .... the wires to the terminal.
4 .... the wood to the wall.
5 .... the papers together and .... them to the board.
6 .... the bracket to the floor.
7 .... the paste all over the paper.
8 .... the cement.
9 .... the bike to the lamp post and .... the chain.
10 .... the hinge to the door.

13 *What's it for?*

Explaining use

1 Look at this kit for surviving outdoors. Match the words to the correct picture.

☐ dental floss   ☐ plaster*

☐ lighter   ☐ razor blade

☐ compass   ☐ mirror

☐ whistle   ☐ torch

☐ tea bag   ☐ plastic bag

☐ aspirin

plaster **BrE** – band aid **AmE**

2 Find something for:

1 starting fires
2 keeping things dry
3 stopping headaches
4 cutting things
5 putting on cuts
6 finding the way.

Example
The lighter's for starting fires.
The … is for keeping things dry.

3 What are the other things for?

4 Listen and check your answers.

5 Complete the sentences with words from the list.

seeing	putting on	making
tying	signalling	

1 The dental floss is for .... things together. It's very strong and useful.
2 The torch is for .... at night and also for signalling.
3 The mirror is for .... in the day and the whistle is for .... a noise.
4 The tea bag is for a hot drink and also for .... insect bites.

6 Work with another student. Ask and answer questions about the survival kit.

A *What's the plaster for?*
B *It's for putting on cuts.*

A *What's the … for?*
B *It's for … -ing …*

7 Work with some other students. Imagine you are going on a trip to the moon. Think of ten things to take with you. Make a list (you can use a dictionary). What is everything for?

Example
oxygen – for breathing
a radio transmitter – for calling home

8 Read your list to the class. Say what things are for.

Example
We have a camera for photographing the earth.

9 Work with a partner. **A** – use the information below. **B** – use the information in file 30 on page 111.

down **across**

A
There are no clues to this crossword. Your partner has the words you need and you have the words your partner needs. You can't say the missing words. You have to describe things.

Example
B *What's 1 across?*
A *It's for building walls.*
B *Bricks?*
A *No, it's soft and grey.*
B *Cement?*
A *That's right.*

Explaining functions

1 Do you have any remote controls at home? What devices can remote controls operate (for example, videos, garage doors)? What devices can you operate with this remote?

Universal remote control

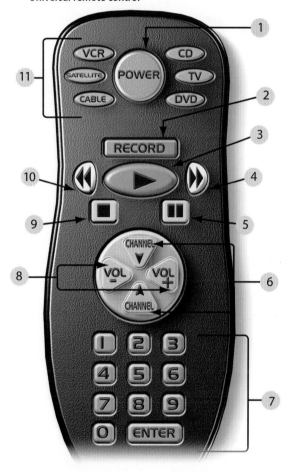

2 Write the numbers of the keys in the function chart.

Key(s)	Function	Key(s)	Function
1	turns the power on and off		stops
	selects a device		pauses
	records		increases and decreases the volume
	rewinds		
	plays tapes, CDs, and DVDs		changes the channel
	fast forwards		enters numbers

3 Work with a partner. Point at different buttons and ask and answer questions.

Example
A *What does this button do?*
B *It turns the power on and off.*

A *What do these buttons do?*
B *They change the channel.*

4 (13.2) Listen to some people programming the remote. Do they have any problems?

5 (13.2) Here are some written instructions for programming the remote. They are in the wrong order. Write the correct number in the boxes. Listen again and check your answers.

PROGRAMMING

[ ] Press **TV** and wait for the flashing red light.

[ ] Press **ENTER**. A flashing light means programming is successful.

[ ] Turn on the television.

[1] Locate the correct code in the manual.

[ ] Type in the code using the key pad.

6 Who says these things, the man or the woman?

	Man	Woman
1 How do you programme this remote?	☐	☐
2 **Pass** it to me. I'll do it.	☐	☐
3 I already have the **code**. It's oh eight oh.	☐	☐
4 Press the TV **button** on the remote. **Hold it down**.	☐	☐
5 It's **going on and off**. Now what?	☐	☐
6 **Key in** the code.	☐	☐
7 **That's it**.	☐	☐
8 But that's **easy**!	☐	☐

7 Look at the words and phrases in **bold** in **6**. Think of other ways to say these things.

8 Match the words and phrases in **bold** in **6** with the words and phrases in the list.

    a number
    b we're finished
    c type in
    d not difficult
    e give
    f don't release it
    g key
    h flashing

9 What electronic devices do you have with you now? For example:

a mobile phone
a laptop computer
a PDA (Personal Digital Assistant)
a watch
a pager
a cassette recorder
an MP3 player

Brainstorm different questions to ask about them. Start your questions with *How do you …?*

Example
a mobile phone
How do you make a call?
How do you pick up messages?
How do you send a text message?
How do you …?

10 Show some other students an electronic device. Explain the controls.

Example
A *How do you turn the power on?*
B *Press the red circular button.*
C *What does this button do?*
B *It moves the menu up and down.*
D *How do you pick up your messages?*
B *Key in the number …*

Listing things

1 Identify the things in the picture. Say what each one is for.

There's an electric drill. It's for making holes.

2 Play a memory game. Close your books and try to remember everything in the picture. Make a list. Write sentences beginning:

There's a …
There's some …
There are some …

Reporting damage

1 Three things were wrong with this shipment. What were they? Read the email and find out.

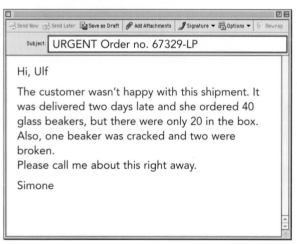

> | Send Now | Send Later | Save as Draft | Add Attachments | Signature ▾ | Options ▾ | Rewrap |
>
> Subject: URGENT Order no. 67329-LP
>
> Hi, Ulf
>
> The customer wasn't happy with this shipment. It was delivered two days late and she ordered 40 glass beakers, but there were only 20 in the box. Also, one beaker was cracked and two were broken.
> Please call me about this right away.
>
> Simone

2 Read Ulf's reply.

1 Was the shipment delayed?
2 How many boxes were there?
3 Were the beakers in good condition?

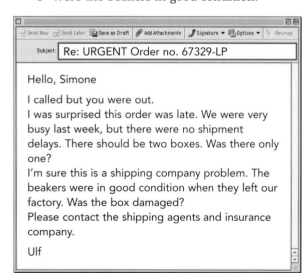

> | Send Now | Send Later | Save as Draft | Add Attachments | Signature ▾ | Options ▾ | Rewrap |
>
> Subject: Re: URGENT Order no. 67329-LP
>
> Hello, Simone
>
> I called but you were out.
> I was surprised this order was late. We were very busy last week, but there were no shipment delays. There should be two boxes. Was there only one?
> I'm sure this is a shipping company problem. The beakers were in good condition when they left our factory. Was the box damaged?
> Please contact the shipping agents and insurance company.
>
> Ulf

3 When is it *was* and when is it *were*? Complete the rules by writing *was* and *were* in the correct space.

> ### *was* and *were*
>
> The verb *be* has two past forms.
> Use .... with I, *he*, *she*, and *it*.
> Use .... with *we*, *you*, and *they*.
> Use *not* to make negatives: *wasn't* (*was* + *not*), *weren't* (*were* + *not*).

4 Complete Simone's next email to Ulf. Use *was* or *were*.

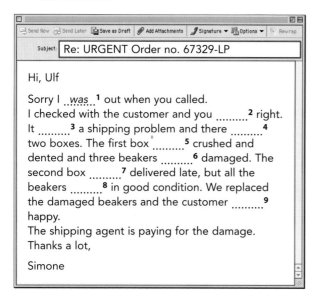

Subject: Re: URGENT Order no. 67329-LP

Hi, Ulf

Sorry I ..*was*..¹ out when you called.
I checked with the customer and you ....² right.
It ....³ a shipping problem and there ....⁴
two boxes. The first box ....⁵ crushed and
dented and three beakers ....⁶ damaged. The
second box ....⁷ delivered late, but all the
beakers ....⁸ in good condition. We replaced
the damaged beakers and the customer ....⁹
happy.
The shipping agent is paying for the damage.
Thanks a lot,

Simone

5 Here are some more things that should be replaced. Think of other things that can be *rusty*, *worn*, *dented*, etc.

rusty bolts   worn belt   dented bumper

crushed boxes   flat batteries   torn strap

cracked glass   bent blade   scratched lenses

chipped plates   leaking pipe   broken leg

6 Work with a partner. Make up conversations about the pictures.

Example
A We replaced the bolts.
B What was wrong with them?
A They were rusty.

A We replaced the belt.
B What was wrong with it?
A It was worn.

7 Work with a partner.
A – use the information below.
B – use the information in file 22 on page 108.

A
You took your car to **B**'s garage and this is the bill. It's too high! Read all the items and ask **B** to explain them.

Example
You 'Windscreen, four hundred euros'?
B   Yes, we replaced the windscreen.
You What was wrong with it?
B   It was cracked.
You 'Front tyres, three hundred euros'?
B   Yes, we replaced the front tyres.
You What was wrong with them?
B   They were …

1st Garage
Surrey Quays Branch

ITEM	COST
Windscreen	€400
Front tyres	€300
Back tyre	€100
Front door	€350
Mirrors	€200
Door handle	€250
Windscreen wipers	€180
Bumper	€150
Aerial*	€60
Headlights	€50

----

aerial **BrE** – antenna **AmE**

Describing a project

1 Look at the pictures of a construction project.
Write the correct number next to the events in the table.

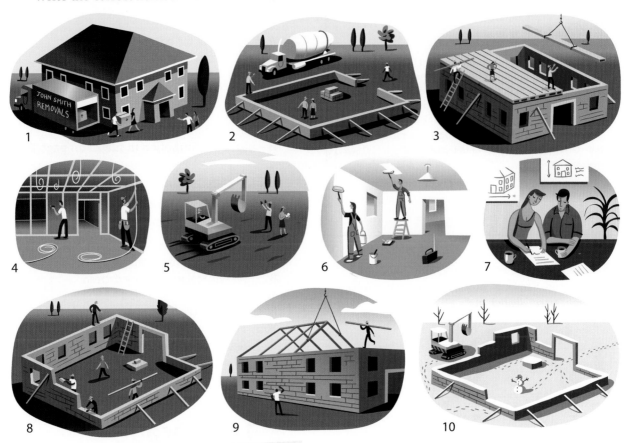

Event	Picture number	When
Signing the contract	7	31 October
Preparing the site		
Starting work on the foundations		
Stopping work because of snow		
Constructing the walls		
Adding the second floor		
Erecting the roof		
Installing the wiring and interior walls		
Finishing the painting		
Client moving in		

2 Read about the project and complete the table with the times.

We signed the contract on 31 October and started work right away. We prepared the site in November and started work on the foundations in December. But then it snowed at Christmas and all work stopped. The snow melted at the end of January and we constructed the walls. We needed to work fast. In February, we added the second floor and erected the roof and then we installed the wiring and interior walls at the beginning of March. We worked seven days a week because the client wanted to move in on Monday, 18 March. We finished painting at 7 p.m. on 17 March and the client moved in on time. It was a rush job, but we did it.

3 We use *in*, *on*, and *at* with different times. Find examples in the story and add them to the rules.

on + dates	.on 31 October.
in + months	....
at + special holidays	....
at + beginnings and ends	....
on + days of the week	....
at + clock times	....

4 Complete these time expressions using *in*, *on*, or *at*.

1 .... 3 o'clock
2 .... 8 July
3 .... the start of May
4 .... Tuesday
5 .... Easter
6 .... September
7 .... 6 September
8 .... the end of the year
9 .... the weekend

5 Complete the story of another construction project using *in*, *on*, or *at*.

It took six weeks to design and construct this building. We signed the contract ....¹ the end of February and the client moved in today. Modular construction is very fast!

We designed the building ....² March. The client's architect worked with our designers and engineers and they finished the plans ....³ Easter. We started construction work after the holiday, ...⁴ 1 April.

The weather was no problem because we constructed the modules inside our factory. It only took seven days. We finished ....⁵ Wednesday last week and ....⁶ nine o'clock ....⁷ Thursday morning we loaded the modules onto trucks and delivered them to the site. We assembled them in only three days.

6 (14.1) Listen to the pronunciation of some verbs from the stories. They all end -*ed*. Is it a short sound or a long sound? Tick (✓) the correct box.

	short	long
signed	☐	☐
started	☐	☐
prepared	☐	☐
snowed	☐	☐
melted	☐	☐
needed	☐	☐
stopped	☐	☐
loaded	☐	☐
constructed	☐	☐
installed	☐	☐
added	☐	☐
erected	☐	☐
delivered	☐	☐
painted	☐	☐
finished	☐	☐
moved	☐	☐

Look at the verbs that end with a long sound. What letters do they end with?

Past Simple: regular verbs

Regular Past Simple verbs end with -*ed*.
This is a long sound if the verb ends with a /t/ or /d/ sound.
It is a short sound with other verbs.

7 Work with a partner. Use the table in **1** to talk about the first project again.
A – say what happened.
B – ask when that was.

Example
A *First they signed the contract.*
B *Was that on 31 October?*
A *That's right. Then they prepared the site.*
B *Was that in December?*
A *No, in November. Then they started work on …*

British and American dates

Be careful how you write dates. The day and the month change position in British and American English.
8/7/2004 is *8 July 2004* in British English and *August 7 2004* in American English.

15 *Where are you from?*

Finding out about people

1 How many countries are working on the International Space Station project?
Who is Dino Brondolo? Read and find out.

Today, sixteen countries are members of the International Space Station project: Belgium, Brazil, Canada, Denmark, France, Germany, Japan, Italy, the Netherlands, Norway, Russia, Spain, Sweden, Switzerland, the United Kingdom and the United States. They have a station in space where people can live and work, and where they do research and scientific experiments. Come and meet one of the people working on the project.

This is Dino Brondolo. He's from Asti in Italy. He's a Development Manager and he builds logistics modules. When Dino isn't working, his hobby is making wine. Dino's family has a vineyard and he goes there at weekends. His other hobby is football. His favourite team is Juventus.

'The scientific research is very important, but the teamwork is the most important thing.'

2 Work with a partner. Take turns to ask and answer the questions about Dino.

1 Where's Dino from?
2 What's his job?
3 What does he do?
4 What does he do at weekends?
5 What's his favourite football team?

A *Where's Dino from?*
B *He's from Italy.*

3 Dino is from Italy. He's Italian. What other nationalities are there in the team?

Example
Belgium – There are Belgian people.

4 Here's another member of the team, but some information is missing. Think of words to complete the text. Use your own ideas.

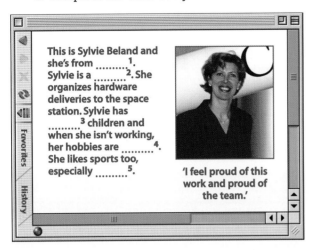

This is Sylvie Beland and she's from .... 1. Sylvie is a .... 2. She organizes hardware deliveries to the space station. Sylvie has .... 3 children and when she isn't working, her hobbies are .... 4. She likes sports too, especially .... 5.

'I feel proud of this work and proud of the team.'

5 Here's the missing information, but it's in the wrong order. Put it in the right place in the text.

a reading and gardening
b two
c Canada
d tennis, swimming, jogging, and cycling
e mechanical engineer

6 If a–e are the answers, what are the questions?

Example
reading and gardening → What are Sylvie's hobbies?

7 Work with a partner.
A – look at the information here.
B – look at file 28 on page 111.

A
1 Here's some information about Takayoshi Nishikawa, another member of the International Space Station team. Answer your partner's questions.

2 Ask your partner questions and complete this information about Robert Curbeam.

8 Imagine a new person is joining your team at work. Prepare some questions to ask them. Use these words.

What / name? *What's your name?* ....
Where / from? ....
What / job? ....
have children? *Do you have any children?*
(Yes.) How many? *How many do you have?*
have a hobby? ....
(Yes.) What? ....
Which sports / like? ....
What / favourite TV channel? ....
....
What / favourite football team? ....
....
have a nickname? ....
(Yes.) What? ....

9 Work with a partner. Take turns to ask and answer your questions in **8**.

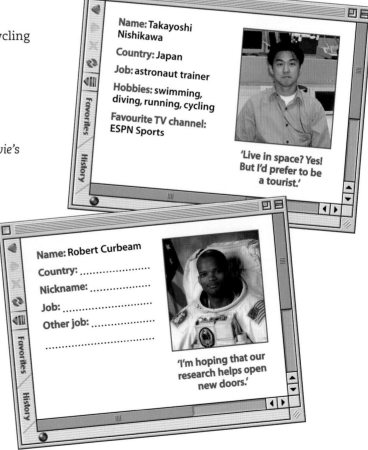

1

Name: Takayoshi Nishikawa

Country: Japan

Job: astronaut trainer

Hobbies: swimming, diving, running, cycling

Favourite TV channel: ESPN Sports

'Live in space? Yes! But I'd prefer to be a tourist.'

2

Name: Robert Curbeam
Country: ....
Nickname: ....
Job: ....
Other job: ....
....

'I'm hoping that our research helps open new doors.'

Countries and nationalities

1 Which country are you from? What's your nationality? Which language(s) do you speak?

*I'm from **Switzerland**. I'm **Swiss**.*

country — nationality

*I speak **French**, **German**, and **Italian**.*

languages

2 Complete the table with words from the list.

Australian	German	the Netherlands
French	Japanese	Italian
Brazil	Argentina	Korean
Canadian	Sweden	the United States
Portugal	Spain	Thailand
Belgium		

Country	Nationality
France	
	Spanish
	Belgian
Korea	
	Brazilian
Italy	
Canada	
	Swedish
	Thai
	Argentinian
Australia	
Japan	
	Portuguese
	American
Germany	
	Dutch

3 What languages do people speak in these countries?

Statistics

1 Say these statistics.

1	2%	3	70%	5	1.3%
2	21%	4	79%		

Example
2% *two per cent*

2 Complete the text with the numbers in **1**. Use each number once.

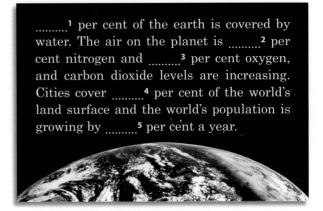

..........¹ per cent of the earth is covered by water. The air on the planet is ....² per cent nitrogen and ....³ per cent oxygen, and carbon dioxide levels are increasing. Cities cover ....⁴ per cent of the world's land surface and the world's population is growing by ....⁵ per cent a year.

3 (15.1) Listen and check your answers.

4 (15.2) Listen and complete another text. This time write the fractions.

..........¹ of the world's population lives in cities. People in cities use ....² of the world's energy. ....³ of the world's energy is used for transport, and cars use half of that. ....⁴ of the world's cars are in Western Europe and North America.

Saying fractions

½	(a) half	¹⁄₁₀	a tenth
⅓	a third	⅔	two-thirds
¼	a quarter	¾	three-quarters
⅕	a fifth	⁹⁄₁₀	nine-tenths

5 Say these percentages as fractions.

1	25%	4	75%	7	20%
2	50%	5	90%	8	66.66%*
3	33.33%*	6	10%		

Example
25% is a quarter

* We say the number is *recurring*. Example
thirty-three point three three recurring

6 What's your first language? Can you speak more than one language? (If you can, what's your second language?) Read the article.

1 How many people speak your language?
2 How many people speak English as a first language?
3 How many people speak English as a second language?

THE WORLD'S MAJOR LANGUAGES	
(first language speakers – millions)	
Chinese	**1,113**
English	**372**
Hindi/Urdu	**316**
Spanish	**304**
Arabic	**201**
Portuguese	**165**
Russian	**165**
Bengali	**125**
Japanese	**123**
German	**102**
French	**70**
Italian	**57**

Chinese is the world's top language. There are about six billion people in the world and eighteen per cent speak Chinese. Around six per cent speak English as a first language. But another six per cent speak English as a second language. And millions more can speak a little English. Roughly a quarter of the world's population speaks some English. English is the international language of science and technology.

7 Find three words in the article that mean *approximately* (~).

8 Work with a partner. Practise saying these numbers exactly and approximately.

1	798	5	680,016
2	3,006	6	6,978,321
3	998,891	7	7,000,562,144
4	41,995		

1 A *Seven hundred and ninety-eight.*
 B *So that's roughly eight hundred.*
 A *That's right.*

9 Work with a partner.
A – look at the information below.
B – look at file 25 on page 110.

A

Ask your partner for the missing statistics and write them down. Answer your partner's questions. Which statistics are the most interesting?

WORLD POPULATION STATISTICS

1 How many babies are born each second?

......

2 How many people die each second? 3

Source: Musée National d'Histoire Naturelle, Paris, 2001

3 How many people are:
14 or younger? ...... %
15 to 59? 60 %
60 or older? 10 %

Source: United Nations world population prospects, 2000

4 How many people are:
male? ......
female? 3,005,616,000

Source: United Nations world population prospects, 2000

5 How many people live in:
Asia? ...... %
Africa? 13 %
Europe ...... %
Latin America and the Caribbean? 9%
North America? 5%
Oceania? 1%

Source: United Nations world population prospects, 2000

6 How many people are:
Christian? ...... %
Muslim ? 22%
Hindu? ...... %
not religious? 14%
other religions? 16%

Source: adherents.com, 2001

7 How many people live on $2 a day or less? 1/3

8 How many people have no access to clean water? ......

Source: United Nations, 1999

Review and Remember 5

Past Simple

was and were

1 Use *was* with *I*, *he*, *she*, and *it*.
  *I **was** late and she **was** early.*
2 Use *were* with *you*, *we*, and *they*.
  *We **were** late and they **were** early.*
3 Change the word order to make questions.
  ***Were** you late? **Was** the train late?*
4 Use *not* to make negative sentences. The contraction is *n't*.
  *He **wasn't** late. We **weren't** ready.*

1 Complete the conversation. Use *was*, *were*, *wasn't*, or *weren't*.

A ....[1] you at the English class yesterday?
B Yes, I ....[2] . Where ....[3] you?
A I ....[4] here, working.
B That's too bad. The class was fun.
A How many people ....[5] there?
B There ....[6] a lot – only five. Why ....[7] you there?
A We ....[8] too busy. One of the computers ....[9] working.
B Oh, dear. What ....[10] the problem?
A A virus.
B Is it OK now?
A No, the hard drive ....[11] damaged and all the files ....[12] lost.
B Which computer ....[13] it?
A Yours.

Work with a partner. Take turns to be **A** and **B** and read the conversation.

Past Simple

Regular verbs in the Past Simple end in *-ed*.

Present – *We look at problems and try to fix them.*
Past – *We look**ed** at the problem and tri**ed** to fix it.*

2 Complete the story. Use words from the list.

| was | were | wasn't | weren't |
| raised | decreased | replaced | called |

A company's million-dollar machine *wasn't*[1] working. The operators changed the fuses, checked the connections, and tested the electronics, but they ....[2] able to find the problem. They cleaned all the parts, refilled the tanks, and installed new belts and rollers. They worked on it for a week but it ....[3] no good. So the managers tried. They increased the pressure and they ....[4] the pressure. They ....[5] the temperature and they lowered the temperature. But the machine still wasn't working, so they ....[6] an engineer. She looked at the machine for one minute and then she pointed to a small part. 'Replace that part,' she said. The operators ....[7] the part and the machine worked again. That's '$50,000', said the engineer. '$50,000 for one minute's work?' said the managers. 'We want to see the bill.' There ....[8] just two items on the engineer's bill. Here's the bill:

Item	Price
Pointing to a part	$1.00
Knowing which part to point to	$49,999.00

3 Read the story again and underline all the other Past Simple verb forms.

Saying when

1 Say the names of the days of the week, the months of the year, and the four seasons. Then complete the puzzle on the right with all the names.

```
T       S           J           F                           D
            W               S
    W   N                           J
        S                       A   A U T U M N
    M       J   Y       S       G   S   M
                    D
A               M
                            O
T               Y
```

Saying dates

We write 15 April or April 15.
We say *the* and *of*: **The** *fifteenth* **of** *April* or *April* **the** *fifteenth*.

2 Work with a partner. Today is Wednesday, 15 April. Take turns to ask what the date is / was:

1 tomorrow
2 last Thursday
3 yesterday
4 the day after tomorrow
5 the day before yesterday
6 next Friday
7 the Monday before last
8 the Saturday after next.

APRIL

M	T	W	T	F	S	S
		1	2	3	4	5
6	7	8	9	10	11	12
13	14	(15)	16	17	18	19
20	21	22	23	24	25	26
27	28	29	30			

A *What's the date tomorrow?*
B *It's April the sixteenth. What was the date last Thursday?*

Preposition or no preposition?

We use *in*, *on*, and *at* with some time expressions.
in December, on Friday, at 9.30

Other time expressions have no preposition.
yesterday, tomorrow morning, last week, this week

3 Complete the sentences. Use *in*, *on*, *at*, or no preposition.

1 The shop is closed ...... Sunday.
2 We start work ...... tomorrow.
3 My birthday is ...... June.
4 They signed the contract ...... last month.
5 We go on holiday ...... the autumn.
6 The meeting is ...... 15 April.
7 I finished ...... 3.00.
8 See you ...... next week.

Numbers

1 Write these numbers in words.

100	*a hundred*
1,000	......
1,000,000	......
1,000,000,000	......

2 Write these words as numbers.

three and five-sixths	......
ninety-three per cent	......
a thousand and nine	......
one thousand six hundred	......
eighteen hundred	......

Hundreds and thousands

We can say numbers like 1,800 in two ways.
one thousand eight hundred or *eighteen hundred*

In American English, you can say larger numbers in different ways too.
two thousand four hundred or *twenty-four hundred*

3 Find the pattern and compare your answers with a partner. Say the missing numbers.

Example
4, 5, 6, ..., 8, ... *seven, nine*

1 13, 15, ..., ..., 21, 23, 25.
2 1%, 2%, 4%, 8%, ..., 32%, ...
3 ...., 1,600, 1,800, 2,000, ...
4 1, 2, 4, 7, ..., 16, ..., 31.
5 ...., 5,555, ..., 3,333, 2,222.
6 20, 10, 5, 2½, ..., 5/8, ...
7 1¼, 2½, ..., 5, 6¼, ..., 8¾.
8 100, 10,000, ..., 100,000,000, ...

16 Can you help me?

Asking for help

1 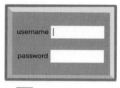 Listen to people asking for help. Number the pictures 1–5.

a ☐

b ☐

c ☐

d ☐

e ☐

2 Listen again and complete the questions.

1 Can I .... that cart?
2 Can you .... me a hand?
3 Can you .... the password?
4 Can I .... your car tomorrow morning?
5 Can you .... the screwdriver?

3 Match the replies to the questions in **2**.

a I'm afraid I can't. I can't remember it.
b I'm sorry, but you're not insured.
c Yes, help yourself.
d I only have two hands, you know.
e What are you trying to do?

4 When do we say *Can I* … and when do we say *Can you* …?

Asking for help

To ask if it's OK to do something, say *Can I* …?
To ask someone to do something, say *Can you* …?

Complete these questions with *Can I* or *Can you*.

1 .... help me?
2 .... smoke in here?
3 .... have a cup of coffee?
4 .... give me a hand?

5 Work with a partner. Take it in turns to ask if it's OK to do different things. Practise saying *yes* and *no* again.

A *Can I make another pot of coffee?*
B *Sure, go ahead.*
A *Thanks.*

A *Can I turn on the heater?*
B *I'm afraid it doesn't work.*
A *OK, it doesn't matter.*

have?

another pot?

close?

turn on?

switch off?

5,000 copies?

sit down?

check my emails?

borrow?

look at?

my friend in Australia?

6 Work with a partner. Take turns to ask and answer these questions. Use the phrases in the boxes below.

1 Can you spell your name for me?
2 Can you tell me your computer password?
3 Can you spell your email address?
4 Can you give me your date of birth?
5 Can you tell me your passport number?

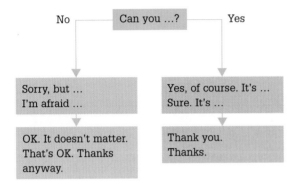

7 When do we say *lend* and when do we say *borrow*?

lend and borrow

When we *lend* we give.   When we *borrow* we take.

Practise lending and borrowing with a partner. Use these questions.

Can you lend me …?
Can I borrow …?

Ask about these things:

– a pen   – a dictionary
– your car   – a mobile phone
– a calculator   – some money

Example
A *Can you lend me your pen?*
B *Yes, sure.*

A *Can I borrow your car?*
B *I'm sorry, but you can't. It's not insured.*

8 Work with one or two other students. Turn to file 24 on page 109 and play a game.

Saying how long

1 (16.2) Listen and complete the label.

CVS Machine Model 24A

OUTPUT: .... pieces per hour

RETOOLING TIME: .... minutes

CLEANING TIME: .... hours

2 Work with a partner. Ask and answer these questions.

1 How long does it take to make 500 pieces?
2 And what about 3,000 pieces?
3 How long does it take to retool the machine?
4 And what about cleaning it?

3 Work in teams and try to answer the questions. How long does it take:

1 to walk a mile if you're walking at 4 mph?
2 to walk to the sun if you're walking at 4 mph?
3 the earth to travel round the sun?
4 the moon to travel round the earth?
5 light from the sun to travel to the earth?

4 Match each answer to the correct question.

a about a month
b 15 minutes
c around 8 minutes 18 seconds
d approximately one year
e about 2,670 years

5 Find out who has the best and worst journey to work. Ask different students these questions.

1 How do you travel to work in the mornings? (by car, train, etc.)
2 How long does it take?
3 How long does it take if the traffic is bad?
4 How long does it take if you travel a different way? (for example, by bus, not car)
5 How long does take if you walk?

How much and How many

1 Look at the first aid kit. Say what's there.

There's a face mask.
There's some insect sting spray.
There are some gloves.

Which things are countable and which things are uncountable? (See page 57 for help.)

plasters

FIRST AID

insect sting spray

alcohol

aspirins

antiseptic cream

bandage

tape

scissors

face mask

gloves

2 (16.3) Listen to one half of a telephone call. What is it about?

3 What does Louisa say? Complete the telephone call.

A Gilles Prost.
B 1 ....
A Hello, Louisa. How are you?
B 2 ....
A Fine, thanks. What can I do for you, Louisa?
B 3 ....
A How much do you need?
B 4 ....
A So that's two bottles of alcohol. Anything else?
B 5 ....
A How many do you need?
B 6 ....
A So that's fifteen bandages. Anything else?
B 7 ....
A OK, I'll send them right away.
B 8 ....
A You're welcome.
B 9 ....
A Goodbye.

4 (16.4) Listen to the whole call and check your answers.

5 Turn to file 26 on page 110.

6 Compare these questions.

How many bandages do you need?
How much tape do you need?

When is it *many* and when is it *much*? Complete the rules by writing *How much* or *How many*.

> **How much and How many**
>
> With countable nouns, we ask ....
> With uncountable nouns, we ask ....

7 Work with a partner. Act out a similar phone call about this order. Ask and answer *How many …?* or *How much …?*

A *I need some alcohol.*
B *How much do you need?*
A *Two bottles.*
B *So that's two bottles of alcohol. Anything else?*
A *Yes, I need some plasters.*
B *How many do you need?*

Item	Quantity
alcohol	2 bottles
plasters	4 packets
bandages	60
face masks	3 boxes
insect sting spray	6 cans
tape	40 rolls
latex gloves	20 pairs
antiseptic cream	8 tubes
aspirins	5 bottles

Packages, containers, and units

We can't count uncountable nouns, but we can count their packages, containers, and units.

some paint
(*paint* = uncountable)
two cans of paint
(*can* = countable)

some money
(*money* = uncountable)
a cent
(*cent* = countable)

8 Complete the phrases with words from the list.

piece	barrel	glass	tube	bag
packet	box	can	sheet	roll

1 a .... of water
2 a .... of sand
3 a .... of tissues
4 a .... of wood
5 a .... of chewing gum
6 a .... of oil
7 a .... of tape
8 a .... of insect spray
9 a .... of paper
10 a .... of toothpaste

Calculations

1 Match the symbols to what we say.

1 **+**   2 **=**   3 **x** or *   4 **−**   5 **/** or ÷

a multiplied by   d divided by
b minus   e equals
c plus

2 Complete these equations with one of these symbols: **+, x, −, ÷**.

a 8 ☐ 4 = 2   c 7 ☐ 12 = 19
b 15 ☐ 5 = 10   d 6 ☐ 2 = 12

Say the equations.

Example
Eight divided by four equals two.

3 (16.5) Listen to some sums and write them down. What number is **n** in each one?

Example
3 x n = 12 (n = 4)

4 Write some sums. Then work with a partner. **A** – dictate a sum. **B** – write it down and say the answer.

Example
A *Nine multiplied by three, minus six, plus four equals …*
B *It equals twenty-five.*

17 *Keep moving*

Describing direction

The road runs **up** a hill, **down** a hill, **through** a tunnel, **between** some trees, **round** a bend, **under** a bridge, **over** a river and **along** a beach.

1 Look at the picture and write the correct number next to the items on the list.

- ☐ hill
- ☐ tunnel
- ☐ beach
- ☐ bend
- ☐ river
- ☐ bridge
- ☐ trees

2 Look at the words in **bold** in **1**. Match each one to the correct diagram.

1 .... 2 .... 3 .... 4 ....

5 .... 6 .... 7 .... 8 ....

3 Use each word once to complete these sentences.

1 The earth travels .... the sun.
2 Go .... the corridor and turn right.
3 You have to fly .... the Sonora desert to get to Los Angeles.
4 A shuttle bus runs .... the factory and the station.
5 Some metro trains run on the surface, but most travel .... ground.
6 Climb in .... the window.
7 What's red and goes .... and ....? A tomato in an elevator.

1 He's .... up and she's .... down.

2 He's .... through the door and she's .... through the door.

3 He's .... round the bend and she's .... round the bend.

4 What's happening in these pictures? Complete the sentences with *coming* or *going*.

5 When is it *come* and when is it *go*? Complete the rules with *come* or *go*.

> ### come and go
>
> We use .... when people are moving in our direction. For example, '.......... here'.
> We use .... when people are moving away from us. For example, '.......... away'.

6 What can you see in this storeroom? Find:

a ladder	a fan
some steps	a chain
a cart	a water fountain
a cardboard box	three plugs
a tube	a boot

Where are they?

7 Work with a partner.
A – look at the information below.
B – look at file 31 on page 112.

A

1 Your partner wants to know where the blue cable goes. Start at the blue plug and tell them. They will draw it on their picture.
2 Ask your partner where the red cable goes and draw it on your picture. Start at the red plug.
3 Draw another cable from the green plug to the water fountain. Take it all round the room. Then tell your partner where it goes so they can draw it.

Getting around

1 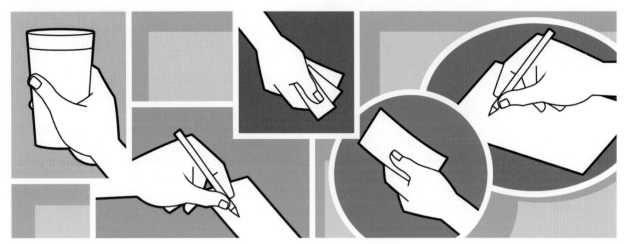 Listen to five conversations. Where are the people in each one?

2 Listen to conversation 1 again. Complete the conversation.

A A ....¹ to Oxford, please.
B Single or ....²?*
A Single.
B That's £30.50.
A Which ....³ is it?
B ....⁴ nine.
A Thanks.

single **BrE** – one way **AmE**
return **BrE** – round trip **AmE**

3 Work with a partner.

1 Read the conversation with your partner. Which British English words do the people use?
2 Move the location to an American station. Read the conversation again with American words.

4 Listen to conversation 2 again.

1 Where is the man going?
2 How many forms are there?
3 What colour is the immigration form?
4 Where are the instructions?
5 What colour is the other form?
6 What's it for?
7 What does the man need to do?

5 **Fill in** a form is British English. **Fill out** a form is American English. Here are some more British words and phrases. What's the American word or phrase?

1 a mobile phone _a cell phone_
2 a lead ....
3 a torch ....
4 anti-clockwise ....
5 autumn ....
6 one thousand eight hundred ....
7 petrol ....
8 aluminium ....
9 6/7/2004 ....
10 Z (zed) ....

6 Listen to conversation 3 again.

1 How much is the ride?
2 Which receipt is correct?

a

Receipt
Date: _21 May_
From: _City_
To: _Excel EC_
Fare: _£16.00_
Signature: _Rm_

Date: _21 May_
From: _City_
To: _Excel EC_
Fare: _£13.40_
Signature: _Rm_

Receipt

b

3 What's the tip?

Do you tip in taxis? Where else do you tip? How much do you tip?

7 Practise saying *receipt*. Which letter is silent? Say some more English words with silent letters. Which letters are silent?

ans~~w~~er	write	know	scissors
half	listen	high	business
knob	scientist	chemist	

8 (17.1) Here are the questions from conversation 4. Listen again. What are the answers?

1 Is there just the one bag?
2 Does it contain any electrical items?
3 Has anyone given you anything to carry?
4 Did you pack your bag yourself?
5 Has it been in your possession at all times?

9 Here are some more questions they can ask at check-in. What are your answers?

1 Do you just have one case?
2 Did anyone ask you to carry anything for them?
3 Who packed your case?
4 Have you had your case with you since you packed it?
5 Are you carrying anything with batteries?
6 How many bags do you have?
7 Did anyone help you pack?
8 Are you carrying anything for somebody else?
9 What electrical items are you carrying?
10 Have you left your bag unattended at any time?

10 Work with a partner. Take turns to ask and answer the questions in **9**.

11 (17.1) Here is conversation 5, but it's in the wrong order. Number the sentences in the correct order. Then listen again and check your answers.

- [ ] What kind do you want? They have Kronenbourg, Heineken, …
- [ ] No, let me get this.
- [ ] Kronenbourg is fine.
- [ ] No, no, you can get the next one.
- [1] What do you want to drink?
- [ ] OK. A pint of lager, please.

12 Work with some other students. Imagine you are in a pub. Act out some similar conversations.

Reading instructions

1 Here's a device for the car. Is it for:

- making coffee on long trips?
- removing air pollution inside the car?
- doing something else? (what?)

What is it? Read the instructions and find out.

How to remove a flat tyre with the automatic jack

1 Start in the normal way by removing the hub cap.

2 Use a socket wrench to loosen the nuts. Turn them anti-clockwise*.

3 Locate the car's cigarette lighter socket. Plug in the jack's cable and position the jack under the car.

4 This is the fun part. The jack's remote control is on the key ring. Press the 'up' button to raise the car.

5 Take off the nuts and remove the old wheel.

anti-clockwise **BrE** – counter-clockwise **AmE**

2 Match the words with the items in the picture.

| hub cap | wrench | socket |
| nuts | wheel | tyre |

3 To put a new wheel on the car, you have to reverse the instructions. What do you do?

1

2

3

4

5

4 Complete the instructions with words from the list.

lower	*put on*	tighten
down	disconnect	clockwise
replace		

Instructions

1 ...*Put on*... the new wheel and .... the nuts.

2 Press the '................' button on the remote control and .... the car.

3 Remove the jack and .... the cable.

4 Use the wrench to .... the nuts. Turn them ....

5 Put the hub cap on.

Two-part verbs

Some verbs have two parts. For example, *put on*, *take off*.
We can usually separate the parts.
Put on the hub cap. or **Put the hub cap on**. or **Put it on**.
Take off the hub caps. or **Take the hub caps off**. or **Take them off**.

5 Separate the verbs.

Example
Take off the hub cap. → Take it off.

1 Plug in the cables. → ....
2 Lift up the car. → ....
3 Pick up the wrench. → ....
4 Throw away the old tyres. → ....
5 Turn on the engine. → ....
6 Fill up the tanks. → ....
7 Write down the address. → ....
8 Key in the code. → ....
9 Tie up the boxes. → ....
10 Shut down your computer. → ....

6 Here are some more written instructions. What are they for?

Shut your computer down and unplug it. Disconnect the cables. Open the case and locate the sockets for the new memory. Put a container under the sink to catch the water and use a wrench to loosen the nuts on the pipe. Position the memory chips over the sockets at a 45° angle. Next, remove the pipe and clear the blockage. Insert the chips by pressing down and forward. Wash it in hot water. Finally, reinstall the pipe and replace and tighten the nuts. Then close the case, reconnect the cables and reboot your computer. ■ ■ ■

7 Which instructions are for installing more computer memory? Which instructions are for unblocking a pipe? <u>Underline</u> the instructions for installing more memory.

Explaining how

Do X to do Y
Use a wrench to loosen the nuts.
Do X by doing Y
Insert the chips by pressing down.

8 Make different instructions with these words.

Example
Press the 'up' button to raise the car.
Raise the car by pressing the 'up' button.

1 press the 'up' button / raise the car
2 press the 'down' button / lower the car
3 unplug the cables / disconnect the computer
4 wash the pipe in hot water / clear the blockage
5 tighten the nuts / fix the pipe in position
6 visit our website / get more information

Experimenting

1 Match the two halves of these sentences.

1 If you heat a piece of metal,
2 If you cool a piece of metal,
3 If you heat water to 100°C,
4 If you lower the temperature of the water to 0°C,
5 If you heat ice,
6 If you pour some water in a bowl and place it in the hot sun,

7 If you leave a piece of iron in water,
8 If you put sugar in hot tea and stir,
9 If you drop a rubber ball,
10 If you drop a glass ball,
11 If you pull the ends of a piece of rubber,
12 If you set fire to a piece of wood,
13 If you pump too much air into a balloon,
14 If you overload your computer,

Example
If you heat a piece of metal, it expands.

a it boils.

b it bounces.

c it bursts.

d it breaks.

e it burns.

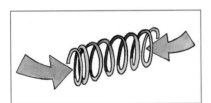

f it contracts.

g it crashes.

h it dissolves.

i it evaporates.

j it expands.

k it freezes.

l it melts.

m it rusts.

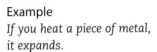

n it stretches.

2 Work with a partner. Test each other. Cover the second parts of the sentences a–m. Take turns to ask and answer questions.

Example
A *What happens if you heat a piece of metal?*
B *It expands.*
A *What happens if you …?*
B *It …*

3 Read some instructions for an experiment. Label the diagram with words from the list.

narrow end	bottle	wide end
piece of paper	shell	rim

What happens

if you place an egg on the rim of a bottle and put a burning piece of paper inside?

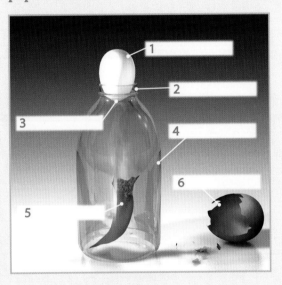

Instructions for the experiment

1 Remove the shell from a hard-boiled egg.
2 Set fire to a piece of paper.
3 Place the burning paper inside the bottle.
4 Place the egg on the rim of the bottle, with the narrow end down and the wide end up.
5 Watch what happens.

4 What do you think happens?

5 Here is a description of what happens, but there are some mistakes. Find the mistakes and correct them.

Example
… *the air* ~~contracts~~ *expands*

'The burning paper heats the air inside the bottle. The air contracts and falls and some air gets out past the egg. The burning paper consumes all the oxygen inside the bottle and the fire goes out. Then the air inside the bottle cools down and expands. That raises the air pressure inside the bottle. And that means the air pressure inside the bottle is higher than the air pressure outside the bottle. That's why the egg falls into the bottle.'

6 (18.1) Listen to the description and check your answers.

7 Work with some other students. Discuss these questions.

1 What happens if you fill the bottle with hot water, then pour the water out and quickly place the egg on the rim of the bottle?
2 What happens if you place the egg on the bottle and put the bottle in 2 cm of liquid nitrogen?
3 If the egg is in the bottle, how can you get it out?

Check your answers in file 27 on page 110.

Instructions

1 Read about some field service management software.
Do you know anyone who uses software like this?

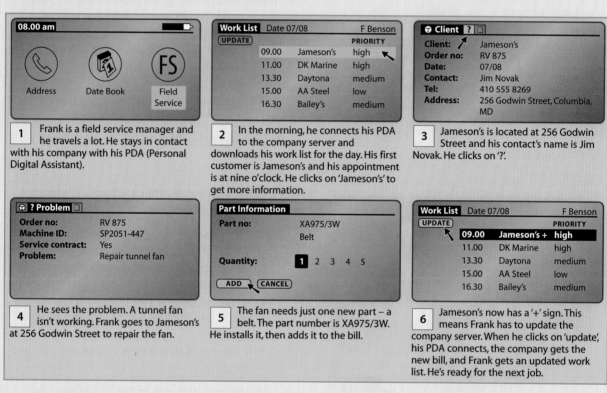

1 Frank is a field service manager and he travels a lot. He stays in contact with his company with his PDA (Personal Digital Assistant).

2 In the morning, he connects his PDA to the company server and downloads his work list for the day. His first customer is Jameson's and his appointment is at nine o'clock. He clicks on 'Jameson's' to get more information.

3 Jameson's is located at 256 Godwin Street and his contact's name is Jim Novak. He clicks on '?'.

4 He sees the problem. A tunnel fan isn't working. Frank goes to Jameson's at 256 Godwin Street to repair the fan.

5 The fan needs just one new part – a belt. The part number is XA975/3W. He installs it, then adds it to the bill.

6 Jameson's now has a '+' sign. This means Frank has to update the company server. When he clicks on 'update', his PDA connects, the company gets the new bill, and Frank gets an updated work list. He's ready for the next job.

2 Use words from the list to complete these instructions.

upload	download	updated	connect
install	remember	click	clicking

Connect ¹ to the company server and .... ² your day's work list. Click on your customer's name to see the contact name and then .... ³ on '?' to learn more about the job. When you make a repair, ... ⁴ to add any new parts you .... ⁵ to the bill. When you complete each job, connect to the company server again by .... ⁶ on 'update'. .... ⁷ the billing information and download your .... ⁸ work list.

3 Use *click* or *clicking* to complete some more instructions.

1 Start the application by .... on 'Field Service'.
2 .... on the customer's name for more information.
3 Learn more about the job by .... on the question mark.
4 To bill the customer for spare parts, ... on 'Add'.
5 .... on 'Update' to connect to the company server.

Quantities

1 Complete the questions. Write *much* or *many*.

1 How _much_ fuel does a jumbo jet use at take-off?
2 How .... seconds are there in a year?
3 How .... steps does the Eiffel Tower have?
4 How .... does it cost to run a refrigerator?
5 How .... people are there on earth?
6 How .... time does it take to download a 1MB file?
7 How .... paint do you need to paint a wall?

2 Match these answers to the correct questions.

a 1,792.
b About five cents a minute.
c It depends on your connection speed.
d A 5-litre can covers about 70 m².
e Around 20,000 litres.
f 31,557,600.
g Approximately six billion.

Two-part verbs

Complete the signs. Use the prepositions in the list.

| up | in | on | off | up | down | away |

Fill the tank _up_ with unleaded petrol after use.

1

Please shut your computer ...... and switch ...... all the lights when you leave the office.

2

Lift ...... the cover to see inside.

3

Don't throw old papers ......
Put them ...... the recycle bin.

4

Check the cable before you turn the power ......

5

Which word?

1 Read the conversations and underline the correct word.

A Hi, Horst. How are you?
B I'm *fine/nice*[1] thanks, and you?

A Can you *say/tell*[2] me the time?
B Yes, it's quarter to three.

A Don't *forget/remember*[3] the password.
B *Lend/Borrow*[4] me your pen and I'll write it down.

A A *single/return*[5] ticket to Blackpool, please.
B When are you travelling back?

A So that's 14 cases of disinfectant. Anything *other/else*[6]?
B No, that's all thanks.

A That's €13.40.
B Can I have a *form/receipt*[7], please?

A Can I *lend/borrow*[8] some money?
B How *much/many*[9] do you need?

2 Underline the word that's different. Why is it different?

Example
screwdriver, wrench, tyre, jack
A tyre is part of the wheel of a car. The other things are all tools.

1 coffee, egg, milk, beer
2 nail, cable, bolt, screw
3 elevator, shuttle bus, bicycle, cart
4 gloves, face mask, wear, boot,
5 earth, sun, moon, fan
6 write, receipt, form, ticket
7 lower, fall, raise, drop
8 water, boil, pour, drink

Maintenance and repairs

1 (19.1) What regular maintenance does your computer need? Listen to a conversation and complete the checklist below. Tick (✓) the completed jobs. What still needs doing?

Maintenance checklist

- ☑ Delete old files, like .tmp and .zip files
- ☐ Empty the Recycle Bin
- ☐ Check the hard drive for errors
- ☐ Run 'Defrag' and 'Disk Cleanup'
- ☐ Download any new service packs
- ☐ Update the drivers
- ☐ Do a back-up

---

2 (19.1) Listen again and complete the sentences.

1 This computer ....
2 I .... some work on it this morning.
3 .... you use the checklist?
4 No, sorry. I ....
5 Then it .... , but we can do it now.
6 .... you .... the Recycle Bin?
7 .... you .... 'Defrag' and 'Cleanup'?
8 .... you .... the drivers?
9 And .... you .... a back-up?
10 I think it .... again.

Past Simple and *did*

Did is the Past Simple form of *do*.
Use *didn't* to make negative sentences and *Did* to make questions in the Past Simple.
I **didn't** *have time.*
Did *you update the drivers?* No, I **didn't**.

3 Work with a partner. Ask and answer questions about another checklist.

A *Did you clean the fan?*
B *Yes, I did.*
A *Did you fill the tanks?*
B *No, I didn't. I didn't have time.*
A *Did you …?*

MONTHLY CHECKLIST

- Replace any worn parts ☑
- Clean the fan ☑
- Clear any blockages ☐
- Fill the tanks ☐
- Oil the wheels ☑
- Adjust the temperature ☑
- Check the alarm ☐

4 What regular maintenance jobs do you do? Are there any jobs you have to do soon? Think of different things that need doing in your life now. Write a list, but don't show your list to anyone yet.

Example
My computer needs upgrading.
The monthly bills need paying.

5 Watch your teacher draw a picture. It's something they have that needs work. Ask questions about it. Find out exactly what needs doing.

Example
Is it a clock or a watch?
Is your watch broken?
Is the strap worn?
Does the strap need replacing?
Can you repair it instead?

6 Use your lists from **4** and take turns drawing. One person draws something on their list. The class asks questions about it.

7 Look at this picture and say what needs doing.

Example
The light bulb needs replacing.
The gate needs fixing.

8 Work with a partner.
A – look at the information below.
B (the owner) – look at file 32 on page 113.

A
Imagine the house in **7** was **B**'s house.
B worked hard last week and they did a lot of the jobs. They fixed a lot of things, but they didn't do everything. Look at the picture and ask **B** what they did.

A *Did you cut the grass?*
B *Yes, I did.*
A *Did you fix the gate?*
B *No, I didn't. I didn't have time.*
A *Did you …?*

Roof
Glass
Tap
Front Door Hinges
EEEK!
Shed
Grass
Dustbins
Flowers
Fuel
Gate
Lawnmower
Mail Box

Offering help

1 What help do these people want?

| c | Can you give me a hand? |

| a | My car won't start. |

| d | Can you do me a favour? |

| e | Are you busy? |

| b | Sorry to trouble you. |

2 Look at these offers of help. Match each one to the correct picture.

Do you want me to:
1 plug it in?
2 open the door?
3 give it a push?
4 hold the torch?
5 take a photo?

3 Work with a partner. Look at the pictures and practise offering help.

Example
A *My car won't start.*
B *Do you want me to give it a push?*
A *Yes, please.*
B *No problem.*

4 (19.2) Listen to a telephone call. Someone has a problem. What's wrong and what help does he want?

5 (19.2) Listen again.
1 What's wrong with the pump?
2 Did Chas check the hoses?
3 What happens if you switch the pump off?
4 What does Tom offer to do?
5 How soon can the engineer be there?

6 Tom asked a lot of questions. Here are Chas's answers. What were the questions?
1 It's the pump.
2 It's leaking again.
3 Yes, they're all OK.
4 It keeps on leaking.
5 Yes, please. How soon can they be here?

(19.2) Listen again and check your answers.

7 Work with a partner. Use this chart to make more calls. Follow the arrows and take turns to speak. Make as many different conversations as you can.

START Tom Parks.	Hi, Tom, this is Chas.	What's wrong with it?	It's leaking again.	Did you check the hoses?
Hello, Tom, Chas here.	Hi, Chas. What's up?	It's the pump.	Did you check the connections?	Yes, they're all OK.
Hi, Chas, what can I do for you?	There's a problem with the pump.	Is it leaking again?	Yes.	What happens if you switch it off?
I think it's the power switch.	What's the matter with it?	No, but there's no power.	Do you want me to send an engineer?	It keeps on leaking.
What happens when you switch it on?	I'm not sure.	Do you want someone to take a look?	Yes, please. How soon can they come?	That's strange.
Nothing at all.	Do you want me to come and take a look?	Yes, please.	Five minutes. I'll send someone right away.	Yes, I know.
There's no green light?	No, nothing.	OK, I'll come right away.	Great, thanks a lot. **FINISH**	I'll send an engineer immediately.

8 Practise making similar calls about some other problems.
A – look at the information below.
B – look at file 17 on page 106.

A
Call 1
Your car won't start. Call a friend for help. Explain the problem and answer their questions.

Call 2
Your friend needs some help with their printer. Find out what's wrong with it and offer to help. Use these questions.

Did you check the …?

What happens when you …?

Do you want me to …?

Safety instructions

1 Read the labels. Which chemical:

1 needs a cool temperature?
2 can't be used near water?
3 needs safety glasses?
4 is poisonous?
5 needs a container with a tight lid?
6 catches fire and burns easily?
7 is dangerous for young people?
8 needs open doors and windows?

2 (20.1) Listen to different people talking about these chemicals. Match each one to the correct label.

3 (20.1) Listen again and complete the sentences.

1 You .... put them on right away.
2 .... lick your fingers and .... drink it.
3 You .... open all the windows and doors when you use it.
4 This box .... get wet. Keep it away from water.
5 .... light matches or cigarettes near this.
6 .... the lid is very secure.
7 .... it in a cool place.
8 .... them to touch this box.

4 Which phrases have similar meanings?

1 You have to do it.
2 Don't do it.
3 You must not do it.
4 You must do it.
5 Never do it.

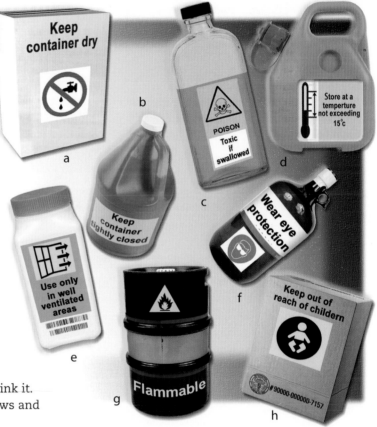

a Keep container dry
b
c POISON Toxic if swallowed
d Store at a temperature not exceeding 15°c
e Use only in well ventilated areas
f Wear eye protection
g Flammable
h Keep out of reach of children #90000-000000-7157

5 Give these instructions in different ways. Use the phrases in **4**.

Example
Keep your goggles on. – You have to keep your goggles on. You must keep your goggles on.
Never drink this. – You must not drink this. Don't drink this.

1 Keep your goggles on.
2 Never drink this.
3 Keep this box dry.
4 Make sure all the windows are open.
5 Don't allow visitors in here.
6 Make sure the lid is secure.
7 Never leave this bottle in a hot room.
8 Don't allow children to touch this box.

6 Read some more safety instructions. Match the instructions to the symbols.

a

b

c

1 Maintain the saw in top condition. Lubricate moving parts and sharpen the blades.

2 Check electric wires and cables for signs of wear.

3 Use a three-pin earthed* plug and do not operate the saw in wet conditions.

4 Disconnect the saw from the power supply before changing the blade.

5 Always use safety glasses when operating the saw.

6 Keep the safety guard in position at all times.

7 Never stand on the saw and don't overreach.

8 Keep children and visitors away from the saw.

9 Do not use the saw when under the influence of alcohol or medication.

 d

 e

 f

 g

 h

 i

earthed **BrE** – grounded **AmE**

7 Here are some similar instructions. Complete the instructions with words from the list.

> keep   oil   allow   remove   unplug
> operate   never   make sure   wear

1 Maintain the saw in top condition. ...Oil... moving parts and sharpen the blades.

2 .... electric wires and cables are in good condition.

3 Use an earthed plug and .... use the saw in wet conditions.

4 .... the saw before changing the blade.

5 .... goggles at all times when using the saw.

6 Never .... the safety guard.

7 .... your feet on the floor and maintain good balance.

8 Do not .... children or visitors near the saw.

9 Do not .... the saw after drinking or taking medicine.

8 Work in groups.

1 Think of more dangerous things that need safety instructions. Make a list.

2 Write some safety instructions for the things on your list.

3 Read your instructions to the class.

Accidents

1 Match the instructions to the pictures. Write the numbers in the boxes.

1 Take a break.
2 Don't bend it.
3 Look where you're going.
4 Don't cut the string.
5 Don't leave that there.
6 Stop pumping.

2 What will happen if these people don't follow the instructions?

Example
He'll fall asleep at the wheel.
The glass will break.

3 Work with a partner. Take turns to be **A** and **B**. **A** – give an instruction from **1**. **B** – question it.

Examples
A *Take a break.*   A *Don't bend it!*
B *Why?*   B *Why not?*
A *You'll fall asleep.* A *It'll break.*

4 (20.2) Listen to some people talking about an accident. What happened?

5 (20.2) Listen again and complete the sentences.

1 I .... an accident.
2 I tripped and .... my leg.
3 .... you be OK?
4 Who .... them there?
5 I .... them there yesterday and .... about them.
6 I .... do it again.

6 Read the sentences in **5** again.

1 Which two sentences are about the future?
2 What's the negative form of *will*?
3 Which four sentences are about the past?

7 Complete this report about the accident. Use the Past Simple form of the verbs in brackets ( ).

Date of accident: 9 June

Time: 10.15 a.m.

Place: The storeroom in the machine shop

Employee: Fernando Sanchez

Description: On 8 June, the employee ..took.. [1] (take) ten 1.5 m steel pipes to the storeroom. He .... [2] (put) eight pipes on the racks, but he didn't finish the job. The telephone .... [3] (ring) and he .... [4] (stop) to answer it. The next morning, he .... [5] (forget) two pipes were still on the floor and he .... [6] (trip) over them. They .... [7] (be) sharp and they .... [8] (cut) his leg. The cut was 40 mm long and it .... [9] (need) a bandage. The employee .... [10] (go) home after the accident but he .... [11] (come) back to work on 10 June. Luckily, he .... [12] (be) OK.

Conversions

1 Do you ever use imperial measurements (for example, inches, feet, pounds)? Who uses them?

2 Read about the Mars Climate Orbiter.

1 What was it designed to do?
2 What went well?
3 What went badly?
4 What height did it need to be?
5 What height was it?
6 What was the communication problem?

The Mars Climate Orbiter was designed to orbit Mars. Its launch on 3 January 1999 went well and so did its trip to Mars. But its landing went badly on 9 September 1999, and something went wrong. NASA lost communication with the Orbiter and it went missing. It needed to be at a height of 85 kilometres (53 miles) or more above the surface of Mars. It was only 60 kilometres (37.5 miles) high. There was a communication problem between two teams of scientists. One team used imperial measurements and the other used metric.

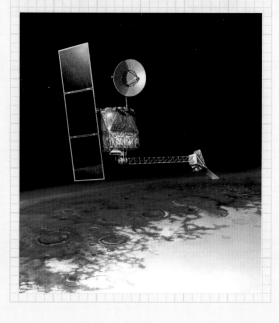

3 Look at these measurements. Which are imperial and which are metric? How do you say them?

1	km/h	9	tonne
2	yd	10	in²
3	°F	11	gal
4	mm	12	kW/h
5	lbs	13	psi
6	m²	14	°C
7	ft³	15	kg/cm²
8	kJ	16	mph

4 Which are units of:

1 speed?   5 temperature?
2 weight?   6 volume?
3 length?   7 pressure?
4 area?   8 energy?

5 (20.3) Listen and complete the conversions.

1 100 mph = ... km/sec
2 1 tonne = ... lbs
3 1 yd = ... mm
4 1 m² = ... in²
5 1 ft³ = ... gal
6 1 psi = ... kg/m²
7 100 kJ = ... kWh
8 0°F = ... °C

6 Work with a partner.
A – look at the information below.
B – look at the information in file 15 on page 106.

A

Ask your partner questions and write the figures. Answer your partner's questions.

Example
What's 400 kilometres per second in miles per hour?

1 400 km/sec = ... mph
2 1,000 lb = 0.4536 tonnes
3 1,000,000 mm = ... yards
4 100,000 in² = 64.52 m²
5 100°C = ...°F
6 1 British gal = 0.1605ft³
7 100 kg/cm² = ... psi
8 1 kWh = 3.6 kJ

Locating parts

1 What's this machine for?

2 Read how the machine works. Write the numbers of these parts in the diagram.

1	ball	4	ropes	7	large spoon
2	chute	5	gate	8	magnifying glass
3	the sun	6	pivot	9	beam of light

The sun rises in the morning and it shines in through the window. The magnifying glass focuses a beam of sunlight and it burns a hole in the bag. Water falls into the large spoon and it rotates on the pivot. This lifts the metal gate and the heavy ball rolls down the chute. The ropes lift the bed up into a vertical position and it drops the man into his shoes.

3 Look for the word *it* in the text in **2**. How many *its* are there? What does each *it* refer to?

Example
… it shines in through the window. (it = the sun)

4 Look at this diagram of a crane. Can you name any parts?

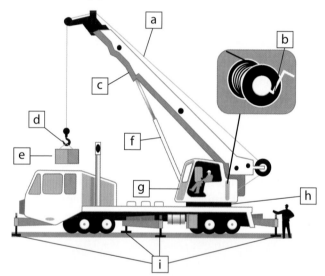

5 (21.1) Listen to someone describing the crane. Match the parts with the words in the list.

operator's cab	load	hook
hydraulic ram	gear	cable lines
outriggers	boom	winch

6 Read listening script 21.1 on page 127. Find the words *it* and *they* in the text. What do they refer to? Complete the rules.

it and *they*

.... refers back to one thing.
.... refers back to two or more things.

7 Write the verbs in the list under the correct diagram.

rotate	lower	burn	blow	roll
pull	drop	push	lift up / raise	

1 ....

2 ....

3 ....

4 ....

5 ....

6 ....

7 ....

8 ....

9 ....

8 Here's another machine. What's it for? Match the parts with the words in the list.

tank of water	magnifying glass	weight
piece of wood	beam of light	pivot
piece of string	piece of rope	lamp

9 Work with some other students. Say how the machine works. Then turn to file 33 on page 114.

10 Work in groups. How are the parts connected in these three machines? Locate parts that are *supported*, *suspended*, or *attached*.

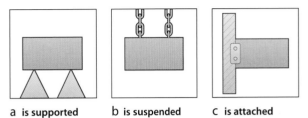

a **is supported**   b **is suspended**   c **is attached**

11 Look back to the first machine in **1**. Use the phrases in **10** to complete the sentences.

1 The magnifying glass .... to the window frame.
2 The bag of water .... from the ceiling.
3 The bed .... by a finger.

12 Look back to the picture of the crane in **4**. Complete the sentences.

1 The hook is suspended from the ....
2 The load is attached to the ....
3 The truck is supported by the ....

13 Look at the automatic window-closing machine. Is anything *supported*, *attached*, or *suspended*? Make sentences with the phrases in **10**.

Describing inventions

1 Look at these inventions. What are they for? How do they work?

a

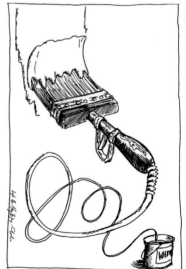

b

c

2 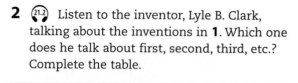 Listen to the inventor, Lyle B. Clark, talking about the inventions in **1**. Which one does he talk about first, second, third, etc.? Complete the table.

	Invention	Picture	What it's for
1			
2			
3			
4			
5			

3 Use words and phrases from the list to complete the sentences. Then listen again and check your answers.

automatic	magnet	takes	map
filled with	*made of*	floats	useful
friendly	puts on	saves	match
pulls			

1 Lyle's coat hanger is _made_ _of_ very thin latex and it's .... helium gas so it ....
2 Lyle often .... odd socks, so this invention is for checking they ....
3 Painting walls .... too long. Lyle's paintbrush is .... and it .... time.
4 Lyle's watch has a .... so he can find his wife in a shopping mall. It's very ....
5 The last invention has a big .... You attach it to a truck and it .... you along. It's environmentally ....

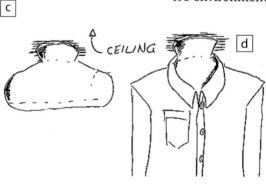

d

e

4 Lyle likes and dislikes a lot of things.

  1 What does Lyle hate doing?
  2 What doesn't he like doing?
  3 What does he love doing?
  4 Do you like doing these things?

5 Work with a partner. Ask if they like doing these things.

shopping
hanging up clothes
shaving
working in your garden
playing football
reading
washing the car
painting and decorating your house
watching TV
cooking
taking the dog for a walk
paying bills
putting the rubbish out
learning English
driving

Likes and dislikes		
?	✔	✗
Do you like -ing?	*Yes, I do.*	*No, I don't.*
	Yes, I love it.	*No, I hate it.*

6 Think of jobs you don't like doing. Make a list.

7 Work in groups. Choose one of the jobs you don't like doing. Invent a machine to do the job for you. Draw a diagram of your machine.

8 Show your diagram to the class and answer these questions.

  1 *What's it for?*
  2 *What parts does it have?*
  3 *How does it work?*

What is it?

This is a puzzle. Read the descriptions. What are they?

Example
It's cylindrical.
It's made of plastic.
It has ink inside.
It's for writing letters.   (It's a pen).

1 It's rectangular.
   It's made of paper.
   It's a kind of book.
   It has words in alphabetical order.

2 It's a rectangular box shape.
   It uses high frequency electromagnetic waves.
   It's a kitchen appliance.
   It's for cooking food quickly.

3 It changes shape.
   It's wet.
   You can drink it.
   It's made of oxygen and hydrogen.

4 It's cylindrical.
   It has two or more lenses.
   It for seeing things a long way away.
   Hubble is a famous example.

5 It's circular.
   It's made of steel.
   It has teeth.
   It's for passing power from one part of a machine to another.

6 It's made of nerve tissue.
   It's soft and grey.
   It controls how you think and move.
   It's in your head.

7 It has a hole (called a *slot*) for money.
   It has an arm on the side.
   It has pictures that spin round.
   It gives you money if you're lucky.

will

+ / –

The contraction of *will* is 'll.
I will help you. → *I'll help you.*
Use *not* to make negatives: *will* + *not* = **won't.**
I **won't** *help you.*   *It won't work.*

1 Write the contractions.

1 I will come right away. ....
2 You will trip. ....
3 She will hurt her back. ....
4 It will not last. ....
5 We will be there at six. ....
6 They will not break. ....

?

Change the word order to make questions.
You'll be OK. → *Will you be OK?*

2 Write the questions.

1 I'll see you tomorrow. ....
2 She'll be late. ....
3 It'll burst. ....
4 We'll set off the alarm. ....
5 They'll be cold. ....

Safety instructions

This is a competition. When your teacher says a number, read and follow the instruction.

1 The red switch has to be on. Keep the green lever down. The blue lever can be up or down. If the controls are correct, sit down. If they are wrong, stand up.

2 The green wire should be connected to terminal 4. The purple wire can be connected to terminal 1 or 3. The black wire must be connected to terminal 2. If the wires are correct, stand up. If the wires are wrong, sit down.

3 The gauge at the top on the left should say 4.0. Don't allow the gauge on the right to fall under 3.0. The gauge on the left at the bottom must not be over 2.0. If the gauges are OK, raise your left arm. If the gauges are wrong, raise your right arm.

4 You can turn knob D to 5 or 7 but never put it on 6. Knob A has to be on 3. Make sure knob B is on 6. Don't touch knob C. If the knobs are correct, put your left hand on your head. If the knobs are wrong, put your right hand on your head.

5 Never turn the machine on when the red warning light is on. Make sure the fan is on. Do not use the machine if the temperature is under 25° or over 35°. Wait for the pressure to increase to 350 before turning the machine on. If it is OK to switch on this machine, put your right hand on your head. If it is not OK, turn round and put your left hand on your head.

6 A must not be inside C. Don't allow D to be in front of C. Make sure you keep E under F. If the diagrams are correct, put your hands on the table. If the diagrams are wrong, shake hands with the person sitting next to you.

Irregular verbs

Find the past forms of these verbs in the puzzle. Read across, down, and diagonally.

H	W	D	W	R	O	T	E	E
A	F	E	I	X	T	H	S	D
D	O	O	N	D	T	O	L	D
C	U	T	R	T	R	U	O	X
M	N	X	X	G	O	G	S	K
E	D	C	N	C	O	H	A	S
A	X	A	L	E	F	T	I	O
N	R	M	X	X	U	X	D	L
T	X	E	S	P	O	K	E	D

go	come	mean	say	rise
can	find	speak	write	think
sell	have	put	forget	do
leave	ring	cut	take	tell

Measuring

1 Complete the table.

2 What measurement tools do you use? What do they measure? What are the units of measurement?

What is it?	a clock	a thermo-meter	a gauge	a tape measure	scales	a volt-meter
What does it measure?	time					
What are the units of measurement?	hours, minutes, seconds					

3 Use words from the list to complete the product specifications.

Tank volume
Length
Voltage
Dimensions
Colour
Material
Operating
Price
Pack sizes
Operating temperature
Width
Pressure
Power consumption
Height
Memory
Guarantee
Speed
Weight
Recording times
Sizes
Software

1 Movie camera

Length : 65 mm
.... : 93 mm
.... : 32 mm
.... : 60 minutes at 15 frames per second

2 Surgical gloves

.... : latex
.... : green
.... : small, medium, and large
.... : 100 pairs per box, 10 boxes per case

3 Flying insect trap

.... : 12.9 in x 11.6 in x 3.7 in
.... : 3.31 lbs
.... : 25 watts
.... : $63.72

4 Air compressor

.... : 12 months
.... : 0.93 gal
.... : 115-60 v
.... : 120 psi

5 Printer

.... : 11 pages per minute (black and white), 8.5 pages per minute (colour)
.... : 4MB built-in RAM
.... : 5°C – 40°C
.... : MS Windows, MS-DOS compatible

Information file

File 1

Unit 3, page 15

Specifying, 7

B

You and your partner both have storerooms.
There are ten different items in each storeroom.
The first person to find them all is the winner.

Find out what's in your partner's storeroom and write it in the correct square. Take turns to ask and answer questions like this:

A *I'll go first. What's in J16?*

B *Nothing! You missed. OK, it's my turn. What's in H18?*

My storeroom

	7	16	17	60	70
G		15 yd rope		4 in bolt	2 m ladder
B		12 ft cable	30 cm screw		
J	60 watt bulb				
P	5 gal pump	10 lb weight			3 amp fuse
Y			6 volt battery		

My partner's storeroom

	8	15	18	50	80
H					
I					
A					
E					
R					

File 2

Unit 1, page 7

Identifying things, 6

1 alarm clock   2 telephone   3 keyboard   4 ambulance

5 email   6 electric drill   7 plane   8 insect

File 3

Unit 2, page 10

One to a hundred, 4

B

Listen to student **A**. When they say one of your numbers, cross it out (3̶8̶).

1 Shout 'Bingo' when you have a line.

2 Shout 'Bingo' when you have all the numbers.

7	16	45	69
11	21	50	71
12	30	61	76
14	38	67	98

File 4

Unit 3, page 14

Specifying, 5

km = kilometre(s)	yd = yard(s)
m = metre(s)	L = litre(s)
cm = centimetre(s)	ml = millilitre(s)
mm = millimetre(s)	gal = gallon(s)
ft = foot / feet	g = gram(s)
(irregular plural:	mg = milligram(s)
1 foot, 2 feet, 3 feet,	kg = kilogram(s) / kilo(s)
etc.)	lb = pound(s)
in = inch(es)	oz = ounce(s)

File 5

Unit 4, page 19

Telephone messages, 7

B

You are Chris Rogers and this is your business card.

Chris Rogers
Quality Technician

Fox Chemicals
68–70 Bardford Road, Jesmond Dene
Newcastle-upon-Tyne, NE2 3JE, UK

Office +44 (0) 191 672458
Mobile +44 (0) 411 69257
Email c_rogers@foxchem.co.uk

Call Teresa Harris at Allied Engineering. If she's not there, leave a message. Ask her to contact you. Give both telephone numbers and your email address.

File 6

Unit 7, page 34

Explaining what things do, 6

A

Here are some industrial robots. Ask your partner for the missing information and complete the table.

Example
What's the maximum reach of Robot 1?
What's the maximum load of Robot 2?

	1 Robot 1	*2* Robot 2	*3* Robot 3	*4* Robot 4	*5* Robot 5	*6* Robot 6
Max. load	5 kg		30 kg		500 kg	
Max. reach		140 cm		150 cm		200 cm

File 7

Unit 6, page 29

Shapes, 1

1 Looking from the top there are six cubes. Looking from the bottom there are seven.

2 Yes, the circle is really circular.

3 Yes, the square is really square. You can check it with a ruler.

File 8

Unit 4, page 21

Checking equipment, 5

B

Your partner needs some things for a job. Tell them if you have them. Tick (✓) the things they need.

File 9

Unit 4, page 21

Following instructions, 3

A

1 Give your partner instructions to draw this picture.

Example

Draw a horizontal line from thirteen to seventeen.

Draw a .... line from .... to ....

1	2	3	4	5	6	7	8	9	10
11	12	13	14	15	16	17	18	19	20
21	22	23	24	25	26	27	28	29	30
31	32	33	34	35	36	37	38	39	40
41	42	43	44	45	46	47	48	49	50
51	52	53	54	55	56	57	58	59	60
61	62	63	64	65	66	67	68	69	70
71	72	73	74	75	76	77	78	79	80
81	82	83	84	85	86	87	88	89	90
91	92	93	94	95	96	97	98	99	100

2 Follow your partner's instructions and draw the lines.

1	2	3	4	5	6	7	8	9	10
11	12	13	14	15	16	17	18	19	20
21	22	23	24	25	26	27	28	29	30
31	32	33	34	35	36	37	38	39	40
41	42	43	44	45	46	47	48	49	50
51	52	53	54	55	56	57	58	59	60
61	62	63	64	65	66	67	68	69	70
71	72	73	74	75	76	77	78	79	80
81	82	83	84	85	86	87	88	89	90
91	92	93	94	95	96	97	98	99	100

What's the connection between your two pictures? (Answer on page 117.)

File 10

Unit 7, page 34

Explaining what things do, 6

B

Here are some industrial robots. Ask your partner for the missing information and complete the table.

Example
What's the maximum load of Robot 1?
What's the maximum reach of Robot 2?

	1 Robot 1	2 Robot 2	3 Robot 3	4 Robot 4	5 Robot 5	6 Robot 6
Max. load		30 kg		10 kg		160 kg
Max. reach	81 cm		243 cm		230 cm	

File 11

Unit 5, page 23

Describing controls, 13

B

Here's another control panel. Your partner has a similar picture, but there are six differences. Describe your control panel to your partner. Find the differences.

A *There are two switches.*
B *Where are they?*
A *On the right at the top.*
B *Are they on or off?*

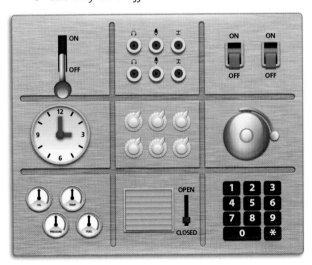

File 12

Unit 2, page 11

Checking an order, 3

B

Some information on this order is wrong. Your partner has the correct information. Listen to them read it and correct the mistakes.

QUANTITY	ITEM	REF. / PART NO.
18	S-hooks	IE-143
16	Size 10 Q-bolts	MTJ/62
12	Spring clamps	Q/236
23	Nylon ropes	Y-742
32	E-clips	URA644
14	Size 40 washers	JSH 21

File 13

Unit 8, page 37

Decimal numbers, 4

B

Ask your partner questions about the missing rates. Complete the table. Answer your partner's questions.

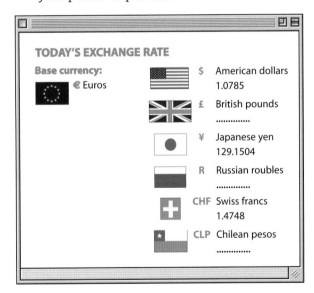

A *I need some ... What's the exchange rate today?*
B *It's ...*
A *OK. That's fine. / OK, I'll leave it, thanks.*

File 14

Unit 7, page 35

Dimensions, 5

B

1 Ask your partner questions about Line Tracker and complete the table.
2 Use the specifications to answer questions about Hyper Peppy.

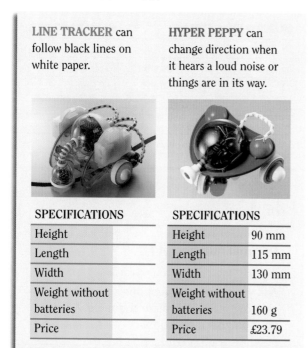

LINE TRACKER can follow black lines on white paper.

HYPER PEPPY can change direction when it hears a loud noise or things are in its way.

SPECIFICATIONS

Height	
Length	
Width	
Weight without batteries	
Price	

SPECIFICATIONS

Height	90 mm
Length	115 mm
Width	130 mm
Weight without batteries	160 g
Price	£23.79

File 15

Unit 20, page 95

Conversions, 6

B

Ask your partner questions and write the figures. Answer your partner's questions.

Example

What's a thousand pounds in metric tonnes?

1 400 km/sec = 894,816 mph
2 1,000 lb = ... tonnes
3 1,000,000 mm = 1,094 yards
4 100,000 in^2 = ... m^2
5 100°C = 212°F
6 1 British gal = ... ft^3
7 100 kg/cm^2 = 1,422 psi
8 1 kW/h = ... kJ

File 16

Unit 8, page 37

Decimal numbers, 4

A Ask your partner questions about the missing rates. Complete the table. Answer your partner's questions.

A *I need some … What's the exchange rate today?*
B *It's …*
A *OK. That's fine. / OK, I'll leave it, thanks.*

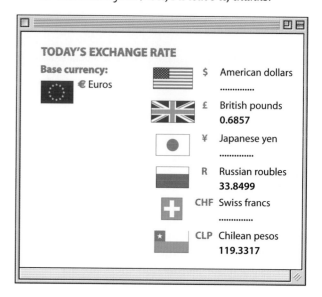

TODAY'S EXCHANGE RATE

Base currency:
€ Euros

$	American dollars	....
£	British pounds	0.6857
¥	Japanese yen	....
R	Russian roubles	33.8499
CHF	Swiss francs	....
CLP	Chilean pesos	119.3317

File 17

Unit 19, page 91

Offering help, 8

B

Call 1

Your friend needs some help with their car. Find out what's wrong with it and offer to help. Use these questions.

Did you check the …?

What happens when you …?

Do you want me to …?

Call 2

You're having a problem with your printer. Call a friend for help. Explain the problem and answer their questions.

File 18

Unit 12, page 57

some and *any*, 6

B

Here is your picture. **A** has a similar picture, but there are twelve differences. Describe your picture to **A** and find the differences.

File 19

Unit 12, page 55

Work tasks, 11

A

Mime all the things you have to do to hang a picture on the wall. For example:

- Marking the position for the nail
- Hammering the nail into the wall
- Hanging the picture on the nail
- Adjusting it so it's horizontal

File 20

Unit 2, page 10

One to a hundred, 4

C

Listen to student A. When they say one of your numbers, cross it out (~~38~~).

1 Shout 'Bingo' when you have a line.
2 Shout 'Bingo' when you have all the numbers.

6	16	48	70
11	17	50	71
13	29	54	83
14	38	67	89

File 21

Unit 12, page 55

Work tasks, 11

B

Mime all the things you have to do to change a light bulb. For example:

- Putting a ladder in the right place
- Climbing up the ladder
- Removing the old bulb
- Screwing in a new bulb

File 22

Unit 14, page 65

Reporting damage, 7

B

You have a garage and you worked on **A**'s car. **A** isn't happy about your bill. Look at the picture and answer their questions. Explain what was wrong with the car.

Example

A   'Windscreen, four hundred euros'?
You   Yes, we replaced the windscreen.
A   What was wrong with it?
You   It was cracked.
A   'Front tyres, three hundred euros'?
You   Yes, we replaced the front tyres.
A   What was wrong with them?
You   They were …

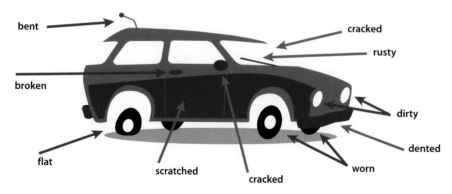

File 23

Unit 9, page 41

Colours, 5

B

1 Listen to your partner and connect these wires.

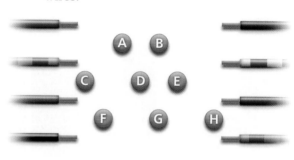

2 Tell your partner how these wires should be connected.

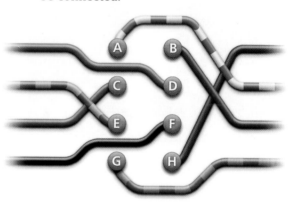

Example
The green and white wire should be connected to terminal A.

File 24

Unit 16, page 75

Asking for help, 8

Play the 'Help!' game.

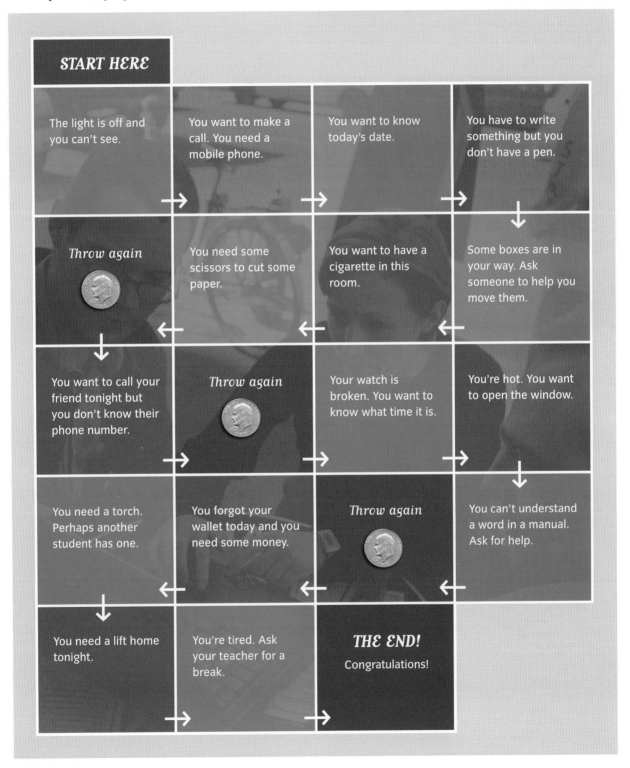

START HERE

The light is off and you can't see. →

You want to make a call. You need a mobile phone. →

You want to know today's date. →

You have to write something but you don't have a pen. ↓

Throw again ↓

You need some scissors to cut some paper. ←

You want to have a cigarette in this room. ←

Some boxes are in your way. Ask someone to help you move them. ←

You want to call your friend tonight but you don't know their phone number. →

Throw again →

Your watch is broken. You want to know what time it is. →

You're hot. You want to open the window. ↓

You need a torch. Perhaps another student has one. ←

You forgot your wallet today and you need some money. ←

Throw again ←

You can't understand a word in a manual. Ask for help.

You need a lift home tonight. ↓ →

You're tired. Ask your teacher for a break. →

THE END!
Congratulations!

File 25

Unit 15, page 71

Statistics, 9

B

Ask your partner for the missing statistics and write them down. Answer your partner's questions. Which statistics are the most interesting?

WORLD POPULATION STATISTICS

1 How many babies are born each second? 5

2 How many people die each second? ......
Source: Musée National d'Histoire Naturelle, Paris, 2001

3 How many people are:
14 or younger? 30 %
15 to 59? 60 %
60 or older? ......%
Source: United Nations world population prospects, 2000

4 How many people are:
male? 3,051,099,000
female? ......
Source: United Nations world population prospects, 2000

5 How many people live in:
Asia? 60 %
Africa? ...... %
Europe 12 %
Latin America and the Caribbean? 9%
North America? ...... %
Oceania? 1%
Source: United Nations world population prospects, 2000

6 How many people are:
Christian? 33%
Muslim ? ...... %
Hindu? 15%
not religious? ...... %
other religions? 16%
Source: adherents.com, 2001

7 How many people live on $2 a day or less?
......

8 How many people have no access to clean water? 1/4
Source: United Nations, 1999

File 26

Unit 16, page 76

How much and *How many*, 5

Try to remember what Gilles said. Write the words.

1 ....
Hello, Gilles. This is Louisa.

2 ....
I'm fine, thanks. And you?

3 ....
We need some alcohol.

4 ....
Two bottles.

5 ....
Yes, I need some bandages.

6 ....
Fifteen.

7 ....
No, that's all thanks.

8 ....
Thanks very much.
....

File 27

Unit 18, page 85

Experimenting, 7

Question 1
The hot water heats the bottle. The bottle heats the air inside and it expands. Some of the air escapes past the egg. Then the air inside the bottle cools down and contracts. This lowers the air pressure inside the bottle, so the egg falls into the bottle.

Question 2
If you put the bottle in 2 cm of liquid nitrogen, the air inside the bottle contracts. This lowers the air pressure inside the bottle and the egg falls into the bottle.

Question 3
Turn the bottle upside down so the egg rolls back to the neck. Blow into the bottle, round the egg. Blowing air into the bottle increases the air pressure inside the bottle and the egg comes out.

File 28

Unit 15, page 69

Finding out about people, 7

B

1 Ask your partner questions and complete this table about another member of the team.

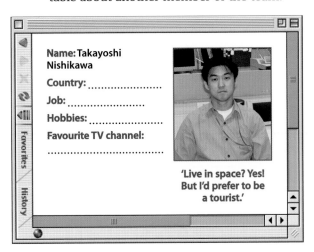

Name: Takayoshi Nishikawa

Country: ....

Job: ....

Hobbies: ....

Favourite TV channel:

....

'Live in space? Yes! But I'd prefer to be a tourist.'

2 Your partner needs information about this member of the team. Answer their questions.

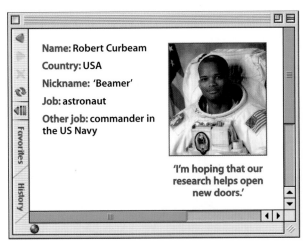

Name: Robert Curbeam

Country: USA

Nickname: 'Beamer'

Job: astronaut

Other job: commander in the US Navy

'I'm hoping that our research helps open new doors.'

File 29

Unit 12, page 55

Work tasks, 11

C

Mime all the things you have to do to build a brick wall. For example:

– Pushing a cart of bricks to the right place
– Unloading the bricks
– Mixing cement
– Building the wall

File 30

Unit 13, page 61

Explaining use, 9

B

There are no clues to this crossword. Your partner has the words you need and you have the words your partner needs. You can't say the missing words. You have to describe things.

Example

A *What's 1 down?*
B *It's for telling the time.*
A *A watch?*
B *No, you see it on the wall.*
A *A clock.*
B *That's right.*

		¹C	²				³C		
		L					A		
		O	⁴P	⁵S	S	W	O	R D	⁶
	⁷P	C							
	L	⁸K	E	Y	⁹R	O	B O	¹⁰T	
	U						A		
	¹¹G	¹²					P		
¹³T				¹⁴ ¹⁵		E	¹⁶S		
O							C		
R		¹⁷H			¹⁸		I		
¹⁹C		A					S		
H		M					S		
		²⁰M	I C	R O	P H	O N	E		
		E					R		
		²¹R					S		

File 31

Unit 17, page 79

Describing direction, 7

B

1 Your partner knows where the blue cable goes. Ask them to tell you and draw it on your picture. Start at the blue plug.

2 Your partner wants to know where the red cable goes. Start at the red plug and tell them. They will draw it on their picture.

3 Draw another cable from the green plug to the water fountain. Take it all round the room. Then tell your partner where it goes so they can draw it.

File 32

Unit 19, page 89
Maintenance and repairs, 8

B

Imagine this is your house. You worked hard last week and you did a lot of jobs. You fixed a lot of things, but you didn't do everything. Look at the picture and answer **A**'s questions.

A *Did you cut the grass?*
B *Yes, I did.*
A *Did you fix the gate?*
B *No, I didn't. I didn't have time.*
A *Did you ...?*

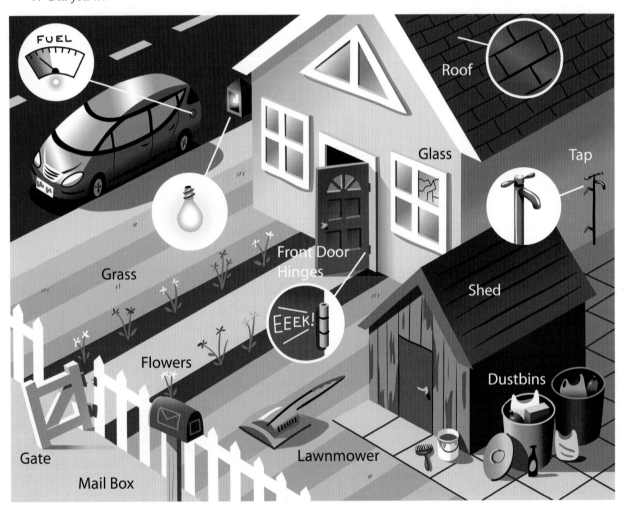

File 33

Unit 21, page 97

Locating parts, 9

Here is a description of how the machine works, but the sentences are in the wrong order. Number them in the correct order.

The automatic window-closing machine
- ☐ and it burns through the rope.
- ☐ and it pushes the switch.
- ☐1 The wind comes through the window.
- ☐ and the weight drops.
- ☐7 The piece of wood rotates on the pivot,
- ☐ It blows the ship across the water,
- ☐ The magnifying glass focuses the beam,
- ☐ The string pulls the window shut.
- ☐4 This turns on the lamp.

File 34

Unit 2, page 10

One to a hundred, 4

D

Listen to student **A**. When they say one of your numbers, cross it out (~~38~~).

1 Shout 'Bingo' when you have a line.
2 Shout 'Bingo' when you have all the numbers.

6	8	45	69
7	21	48	76
12	28	54	83
13	30	61	98

File 35

Unit 12, page 55

Work tasks, 11

D

Mime all the things you have to do to fill a car with petrol*. For example:
- Paying with your credit card
- Opening the tank
- Removing the pump
- Filling the tank

petrol **BrE** – gasoline **AmE**

File 36

Unit 4, page 21

Following instructions, 3

B

1 Follow your partner's instructions and draw the lines.

1	2	3	4	5	6	7	8	9	10
11	12	13	14	15	16	17	18	19	20
21	22	23	24	25	26	27	28	29	30
31	32	33	34	35	36	37	38	39	40
41	42	43	44	45	46	47	48	49	50
51	52	53	54	55	56	57	58	59	60
61	62	63	64	65	66	67	68	69	70
71	72	73	74	75	76	77	78	79	80
81	82	83	84	85	86	87	88	89	90
91	92	93	94	95	96	97	98	99	100

2 Give your partner instructions to draw this picture.

Example
Draw a diagonal line from fifty-six to twenty.
Draw a .... line from .... to ....

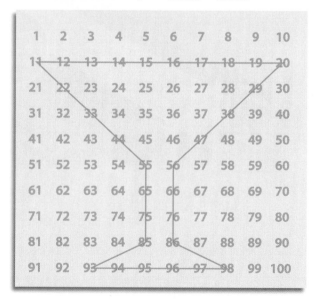

What's the connection between your two pictures? (Answer on page 117.)

Metric–imperial conversions

Length

1 in = 2.54 cm	1 cm = 0.3937 in
1 ft = 30.48 cm	1 m = 3.28 ft
1 yd = 0.9144 m	1 m = 1.0936 yd
1 mile = 1.6093 km	1 km = 0.62 miles

Area

$1 \text{ in}^2 = 6.45 \text{ cm}^2$
$1 \text{ ft}^2 = 0.0929 \text{ m}^2$
$1 \text{ yd}^2 = 0.836 \text{ m}^2$
$1 \text{ square mile} = 2.59 \text{ km}^2$
$1 \text{ cm}^2 = 0.155 \text{ in}^2$
$1 \text{ m}^2 = 10.76 \text{ ft}^2$
$1 \text{ m}^2 = 1.196 \text{ yd}^2$
$1 \text{ km}^2 = 0.3861 \text{ square miles}$

Volume

$1 \text{ in}^3 = 16.39 \text{ cm}^3$	$1 \text{ m}^3 = 35.31 \text{ ft}^3$
1 UK pint = 0.5683 L	1 L = 1.7597 UK pints
1 US pint = 0.4732 L	1 L = 2.1134 US pints
1 UK gal = 4.5461 L	1 L = 0.22 UK gal
1 US gal = 3.7854 L	1 L = 0.2642 US gal

Weight

1 oz = 28.3495 g
1 lb = 0.4536 kg
1 UK ton = 1.016 tonnes
1 US ton = 0.9072 tonnes
1 g = 0.0353 oz
1 kg = 2.2046 lb
1 tonne = 0.9842 UK tons
1 tonne = 1.1023 US tons

Temperature

To convert °F to °C: – 32 x 5 ÷ 9
To convert °C to °F: x 9 ÷ 5 + 32

Abbreviations

cm	centimetre / centimetres
ft	foot / feet
gal	gallon / gallons
in	inch / inches
km	kilometre / kilometres
L	litre / litres
lb	pound / pounds
m	metre / metres
oz	ounce / ounces
yd	yard / yards
°C	degrees Celsius
°F	degrees Fahrenheit

British English / American English glossary

British English	American English
accelerator	gas pedal
aerial	antenna
aeroplane	airplane
aluminium	aluminum
anti-clockwise	counter-clockwise
autumn	fall
cinema	movie theatre
earthed	grounded
extension lead	power strip
flat (battery)	dead (battery)
gear lever	stick shift
lead	cord
lift	elevator
mobile phone	cell phone
motorway	highway / freeway
petrol	gasoline
petrol station	gas station
plaster	band aid
polystyrene	styrofoam
post box	mail box
return ticket	round trip ticket
roundabout	traffic circle
rubbish bin / dustbin	trash can
single	one way
tap	faucet
toilets	bathroom / restroom
torch	flashlight
tyre	tire
windscreen	windshield
zip	zipper

Numbers

Numbers

1	one
2	two
3	three
4	four
5	five
6	six
7	seven
8	eight
9	nine
10	ten
11	eleven
12	twelve
13	thirteen
14	fourteen
15	fifteen
16	sixteen
17	seventeen
18	eighteen
19	nineteen
20	twenty
21	twenty-one
22	twenty-two
23	twenty-three
24	twenty-four
30	thirty
40	forty
50	fifty
60	sixty
70	seventy
80	eighty
90	ninety
100	a hundred

Ordinals

1st	first
2nd	second
3rd	third
4th	fourth
5th	fifth
6th	sixth
7th	seventh
8th	eighth
9th	ninth
10th	tenth
11th	eleventh
12th	twelfth
13th	thirteenth
14th	fourteenth
15th	fifteenth
16th	sixteenth
17th	seventeenth
18th	eighteenth
19th	nineteenth
20th	twentieth
21st	twenty-first
22nd	twenty-second
23rd	twenty-third
24th	twenty-fourth
25th	twenty-fifth
26th	twenty-sixth
27th	twenty-seventh
28th	twenty-eighth
29th	twenty-nineth
30th	thirtieth

Large numbers

100	a hundred / one hundred
1,000	a thousand / one thousand
10,000	ten thousand
100,000	a hundred thousand / one hundred thousand
1,000,000	a million / one million
1,000,000,000	a billion / one billion

Fractions

1/2 a half
1/4 a quarter
1/3 a third
2/3 two-thirds
3/4 three-quarters
9/10 nine-tenths

Decimals

0.5	zero point five *or* nought point five
16.6	sixteen point six
16.16	sixteen point one six
16.06	sixteen point zero six *or* sixteen point oh six

Prices

€ 99	ninety-nine euros
¥ 3,000	three thousand yen
$ 25.50	twenty-five dollars and fifty cents *or* twenty-five fifty

Irregular verbs

Regular verbs end in *-ed* in their past form: *fix* → *fixed*, *work* → *worked*.
But many useful verbs are irregular. Study this list and learn the irregular past forms.

Present	Past	Present	Past
be (am/is, are)	was, were	learn	learnt
become	became	leave	left
blow	blew	lend	lent
break	broke	lose	lost
bring	brought	make	made
build	built	mean	meant
burn	burnt	meet	met
burst	burst	must	had to
buy	bought	pay	paid
can	could	put	put
catch	caught	read	read
choose	chose	rise	rose
come	came	run	ran
cost	cost	say	said
cut	cut	see	saw
do	did	send	sent
draw	drew	shut	shut
drink	drank	sit	sit
drive	drove	speak	spoke
eat	ate	stand	stood
fall	fell	swim	swam
find	found	take	took
fly	flew	teach	taught
forget	forgot	tear	tore
get	got	tell	told
give	gave	think	thought
go	went	throw	threw
grow	grew	understand	understood
have	had	wear	wore
hear	heard	win	won
hit	hit	write	wrote
hold	held		
hurt	hurt		
keep	kept		
know	knew		

The answer to the question in Files 9 and 36 is "Happy Hour".

Listening script

1.1

1   A   Are you Jean-Michel?
    B   Yes, I am.
    A   Hi, I'm Eduardo Santez.
    B   Hello. Nice to meet you.
    A   Nice to meet you, too. Welcome to São Paulo.
    B   Thank you. It's nice to be here.

2   A   Can you speak Portuguese?
    B   No, I'm sorry.
    A   I only speak a little English.
    B   Me too. Just a little, so please speak slowly.
    A   OK. No problem!

3   A   This is for you.
    B   What is it?
    A   It's an electronic pass.
    B   Is it for security?
    A   Yes, it is.
    B   Thanks.

4   A   What's this?
    B   It's for you. It's a manual for your machine.
    A   Thank you.
    B   You're welcome.
    A   Is it in Portuguese?
    B   No, it's in English.

1.2

1   A   I'm here to see Declan Kelly.
    B   He's in room nine six two.
    A   Thanks.

2   A   What flight is this?
    B   It's Air France three three seven.
    A   From Boston?
    B   Yes.
    A   Thanks.

3   A   What's the serial number?

    B   It's three eight four, dash, eight two three five.
    A   Eight two three five?
    B   Yes, that's right.

4   A   Here's the model number.
    B   Is it seven eight three slash six zero?
    A   No, it's seven eight three slash *seven* zero.

5   A   What's your phone number?
    B   It's oh one double two three, that's the area code. Then two seven oh, nine three eight. And my extension number is five four two.
    A   And what's the country code for the UK?
    B   It's four four.

1.3

1   a manual
2   an electronic organizer
3   a pen
4   an apple
5   a mobile phone
6   a passport
7   an English dictionary
8   a bag
9   an electronic pass
10 a map
11 a pencil
12 a torch
13 a key
14 an orange
15 an umbrella
16 a ticket
17 a battery
18 an identity card
19 an alarm clock
20 a newspaper

1.4

(*sound effects*)

1 alarm clock
2 telephone ringing
3 keyboard
4 ambulance siren
5 email arriving
6 electric drill
7 aeroplane
8 insect buzzing

2.1

A This is the English alphabet.
B *And the American alphabet.*
A OK. This is the alphabet in English *and* American. Are you ready? ABC …
B DEF …
A GHI …
B JKL …
A MNO …
B PQR …
A STU …
B VWX …
A YZ …
B We say zee in America.
A Well, in England we say zed.
B It's zee.
A And zed.
B Zee.

2.2

1 I work for IBM.
2 I work for SAP.
3 I work for GEC.
4 I work for TJX.
5 I work for KAO.
6 I work for SHV.
7 I work for BTR.
8 I work for WSY.

2.3

A Good morning.
B Good morning. I'm here to see John Heath.
A What's your name, please?
B It's Maria Badajoz.
A How do you spell that?
B My first name's Maria, M-A-R-I-A.
A And your last name?
B Badajoz, that's B-A-D-A-J-O-Z.
A And what company are you with?
B I work for JYR Technologies.
A JYR?
B That's right.
A Thank you. Please have a seat.

2.4

1 ninety-six
2 twenty-seven
3 eighty
4 eighteen
5 seventy-two
6 fourteen
7 forty

2.5

A OK, this is the order. There are six items.
B All right, what are they?
A I'll read them. Are you ready?
B Yes, ready.
A OK. Sixteen S-hooks, reference number EI dash 983.
B Sixteen?
A That's right, sixteen. Then eighty-five size twelve U-bolts, reference number MTJ slash six two.
B Slash six two. OK, got it.
A Next is seventy-two spring clamps, part number Q eight two three six.
B OK, seventy-two.
A Yes, then I want fourteen nylon ropes. Reference number Y dash nine five eight.
B How many again?
A Fourteen. And sixty-four G-clips. That's WRA double five seven.
B OK, sixty-four G-clips.
A And the last thing is size eighteen washers. I want eighty washers, part number JS slash eight six.
B JS slash eight six?
A That's right. And that's it.
B OK, so that's sixteen S-hooks, reference number EI dash 983 …

3.1

A Hey, Rafael, are you hungry?
B Yes. I need something to eat.
A Me too. Let's get some lunch.
B Good idea!
A Do you want a burger?
B Yes, two burgers, please.
A Two?
B I'm very hungry.
A OK, no problem. They have sandwiches, too, and hot dogs.
B No, just two burgers, please … with cheese … and some fries.
A Small or large fries?

B Large.
A And something to drink?
B Yes, a shake – a medium shake.
A And do you want a doughnut?
B No, thanks.

3.2

S Can I help you?
A Yes, two cheeseburgers and one chicken sandwich, please, and two orders of French fries.
S Large or small fries?
A Large.
S And something to drink?
A Yes, a medium shake, a small coffee, and a large Diet Coke.
S Coming right up.
A How much is it?
S That's eighteen dollars and sixty-seven cents.
A Great. Here you are.
S Thanks. Have a nice day.

3.3

1 A Can I help you?
  B Yes, I want to call my office.
  A No problem. Use my phone.
  B Thank you. I just want to listen to my voicemail messages.
  A That's OK.

2 A Can I have some paper? I want to write down this address.
  B Sure.
  A And I want a map. Do you have a map of Paris?
  B Yes. Do you want to look at a street map or metro map?
  A A street map, please.

3 A Is this your newspaper?
  B Yes, do you want to read it?
  A Yes, I want to check the football results.
  B No problem.

4 A Oh, I'm tired.
  B Do you want a coffee?
  A No, thanks.
  B Do you want to open the window?
  A No.

B Work on a different job?
A No.
B What about a break?
A That's a good idea.

4.1

A Can I have your email address Jean-Luc?
B Sure, no problem. It's J underscore, Luc, that's L-U-C, at redtop …
A Redtop? Is that all one word?
B Yes, one word, then dot co, dot F-R.

4.2

A Research and Development department.
B Hello. Can I speak to Maria, please?
A I'm afraid she's not here.
B Can you take a message?
A Sure. Just a second. I need a pen.
B Are you ready?
A Yes, ready.
B Please ask Maria to call me. This is Don Sinclair.
A How do you spell that?
B D-O-N. Then new word, Sinclair: S-I-N-C-L-A-I-R.
A S-I-N-C-L-A-I-R. Is that correct?
B Yes, that's right. My number is 4989, that's the code. Then 287 9826.
A OK. So that's 4989 287 9806.
B No, 98_2_6.
A 98_2_6.
B That's right. Thanks very much.
A You're welcome. Goodbye.
B Goodbye.

4.3

A Please leave your message after the tone.
B Hi, Chas! It's Marcus. Thanks for your email about installing the network. I'm afraid we have a problem. We don't have enough twenty-five-foot cables. We need four, but we only have three. We have an extra six-foot cable, but that's no good. And we have another problem. We only have one installation disk. I think we need two. Please call me about this. Thanks a lot. Bye.

4.4

1 Draw a vertical line from 68 to 98.
2 Draw a horizontal line from 15 to 16.
3 Draw a diagonal line from 36 to 68.
4 Draw a vertical line from 63 to 93.
5 Draw a vertical line from 16 to 36.
6 Draw a horizontal line from 93 to 98.
7 Draw a vertical line from 15 to 35.
8 Draw a diagonal line from 35 to 63.

5.1

sockets   gauges
switches   levers
knobs

5.2

A OK, Mr Anderson. You have a room for three nights.
B Great. Where's the hotel restaurant?
A On the second floor, but I'm afraid it's closed. It opens for breakfast at seven tomorrow morning.
B What about room service?
A I'm afraid there's no room service.
B Are there any restaurants near the hotel?
A No, sorry. There aren't.
B Is there a minibar in my room?
A No, I'm afraid there isn't. It's room 405, on the fourth floor.
B Is there an elevator?
A Yes, there is.
B Good. Where is it?
A Over there. But it's not working.
B Ah!

7.1

1 This robot has eight legs and it can pull loads of 221 pounds. It can climb up walls too, with its vacuum gripper feet. It's designed to operate in dangerous radioactive environments, like nuclear power reactors.
2 This is the solution for dirty windows. It's made in Germany and it's a window-cleaning robot. It's very fast. It can clean 120 square metres of glass in just one hour.
3 This robot can pick things up, pack boxes, and load goods onto pallets. It's designed to save floor space. It has a maximum load of 150 kilograms and it can carry materials 30 metres.
4 This long robot arm can reach 15 metres and it's designed to operate 240 miles above the earth. Astronauts use it to move things around on the International Space Station.
5 If you have a big garden, you need this robot. It's fully automatic, so you just turn it on and it cuts the grass for you. And how much is it? Only $795.
6 Sony designed this robot and it's an electronic pet. It's only 230 millimetres long, but it can travel over six metres a minute. It can play football and score goals too.

8.1

A Can I help you?
B Yes. My sound card doesn't work.
A OK, no problem. I'll replace it.
B Thanks, and I need to log on to the Internet.
A Do you have a network password?
B Yes, I do, but I need a browser.
A Do you want Internet Explorer or Netscape?
B Netscape.
A OK, I'll install it. Anything else?
B Yes. Do you have software for different printers?
A Different printers?
B Yes. I need to use printers in different buildings.
A OK, you need drivers for the network printers. I'll install them.
B Great. That's it. Can you do it today?
A Today? Oh, no! Sorry, but I'm very busy.
B But I need it for a meeting tomorrow.
A Yes, and I need more time.

8.2

Three point four six.
Twenty three point four.
Zero point eight.
One point oh six.

8.3

1 A Can I help?
  B Yes, I need some Canadian dollars. What's the exchange rate?
  A 1.6031.
  B OK, that's fine.

2 A I need some Mexican pesos. What's the exchange rate today?
  B It's 7.87491.
  A Thanks.

3 A Next?
  B Hi, I need some Japanese yen. What's today's exchange rate?
  A 189.406.
  B Ah, OK. I think I'll leave it, thanks.

9.1

A The lights don't work. I think it's the wiring.
B OK, let's check the connections.
A Right.
B The green and white wire should be connected to terminal A.
A That's OK.
B The blue and orange wire should be connected to terminal B.
A Uh-huh.
B The purple wire should be connected to terminal C.
A Terminal C. Oh, I see.
B Terminal D should be connected to the black wire.
A Uh-huh.
B Then the brown wire should be connected to terminal E.
A Ah, OK.
B And the yellow and red wire should be connected to terminal F.
A All right.
B Do they work now? Turn it on and see.
A Yes. It's OK now.

9.2

VO Pablo is at a customer's site.
Guard Excuse me.
Pablo Yes?
Guard Do you work here?
Pablo No, I'm a service engineer. I work for Allied Engineering. We maintain this machine.
Guard Do you have a security pass?
Pablo Yes, it's here.
Guard Can I see it?
Pablo Sure.
Guard That's OK, then. Sorry about that.
Pablo That's all right. I understand.
VO Ten minutes later.
Man Er, excuse me.
Pablo Yes?
Man Can you help me?
Pablo Sure, what is it?
Man I don't have my security pass and I want to take these computers outside. Can you open the door for me?
Pablo How do I do that?
Man Hold your pass in front of that box. It opens the door.
Pablo OK.
Man That's great. Thanks a lot.
Pablo You're welcome.
VO Two minutes later.
Woman Hi, Pablo. Are you finished?
Pablo Yes, that's it.
Woman Good. ... Hey! Who's that?
Pablo I don't know.
Woman What company does he work for?
Pablo He works here.
Woman No, he doesn't. Does he have a security pass?
Pablo I don't know.
Woman He doesn't work here. But he has our computers. Who is he?
Pablo Oh, no!

10.1

A Are you OK?
B No, I can't find the documentation for the new software.
A It's not behind the door with the other manuals?
B No, and I'm in a hurry. I have a meeting with a customer.
A Is it in a file?
B Yes, a blue file.
A Is it on the shelf between the boxes?
B No, I think it's in a bag. A green plastic bag. This is very bad. The meeting's in

Rouen and it's a two-hour drive.

A What's that next to the radiator?

B It's the bag! Oh, thank you. Thank you very much. Good, now I just need my car keys …

A Car keys … Look, they're under the papers in front of the monitor.

B Excellent! OK, I'm ready to go! What's the time?

A Eleven o'clock.

B Oh, no. I'm late again.

10.2

1 A Can you help me?

B Sure, what's the problem?

A It's this bulb. It's burnt out.

B There's a new bulb in that box over there.

2 A Are you busy?

B No, what's up?

A It's these batteries. They're flat.

B There are some new batteries in those boxes over there.

11.1

A This drill's no good.

B What's wrong with it?

A The battery's flat.

B Why don't you plug it in at the wall?

A I can't. There's no socket here.

B There's a socket over there.

A Yes, but it's too far.

B Then use the extension lead.

A I can't. It's too short.

B Then buy another one.

A That's a good idea … Just one problem. Do you have any money?

11.2

A Sorry, you can't park here. You have to move.

B Where can we park?

A There's a car park down the street.

B But it's full.

A Then you have to use a meter.

B But we can't find a meter.

A Sorry, but that sign means no parking.

12.1

A What are you doing?

B I'm fixing this hose.

A Why?

B Because it's leaking.

A Are you replacing it?

B No, I'm fixing it. It's a very small leak.

A Are you using tape?

B No, I'm not.

A Because tape's no good.

B I know.

A Tape doesn't last.

B I know. I'm not using tape. I'm using a clamp.

A Clamps are better.

B I know. That's why I'm using a clamp.

A OK!

12.2

A Do you have a ruler?

B No, sorry, but there's a tape measure in my bag.

A Can I use that?

B Sure, help yourself. It's over there.

A Thanks.

B Got it?

A No, I'm just looking now. There's some chewing gum in here, and there are some keys.

B That's the wrong pocket.

A Is there any money here?

B No. Keep looking.

A There's a torch, but it doesn't work.

B I know. There aren't any batteries in it.

A Ah, here's the tape measure.

B Good.

A Hey, what's this? It's a sandwich – a cheese sandwich! Ooh, it looks good.

B Put that back! That's my lunch!

13.1

A What's this for?

B What? The dental floss?

A Yes. Is it for cleaning our teeth?

B Yes, if you want. But it's also for tying things together. It's very strong … very useful.

A OK, and we have a torch. That's for seeing

at night, right?

B Yes, and also for signalling – if we want someone to find us.

A Is the mirror for signalling, too?

B Yes, for signalling in the day, and there's also a whistle for making a noise.

A I see. Now the tea bag is for a hot drink?

B Yes, but it's also for putting on insect bites.

A Oh, really?

B Yes. It's good for insect bites.

A Oh …

13.2

A How do you programme this remote?

B What do you want to control? The television?

A Yes.

B Pass it to me. I'll do it.

A No, I want to do it.

B You have to find the right code. It's in the manual.

A I already have the code. It's oh eight oh.

B OK. Turn the television on.

A It is on.

B Then press the TV button on the remote. Hold it down. Don't release it.

A OK.

B Can you see the light in the centre at the top?

A Yes. It's going on and off. Now what?

B Key in the code.

A Where?

B On the keypad … at the bottom.

A Oh … eight … oh.

B Good. Press ENTER. Is the light flashing?

A Yes. Now what?

B Nothing, that's it.

A We're finished?

B Yes, that's it.

A But that's easy!

B I know. Now give me the remote.

14.1

signed	constructed
started	installed
prepared	added
snowed	erected
melted	delivered
needed	painted

stopped	finished
loaded	moved

15.1

70% of the earth is covered by water. The air on the planet is 79% nitrogen and 21% oxygen, and carbon dioxide levels are increasing. Cities cover 2% of the world's land surface and the world's population is growing by 1.3% a year.

15.2

Half of the world's population lives in cities. People in cities use three-quarters of the world's energy. A quarter of the world's energy is used for transport and cars use half of that. Two-thirds of the world's cars are in Western Europe and North America.

16.1

1 A Are you OK?

  B No, these boxes are in the way. Can I move them?

  A Sure, go ahead.

  B Thanks. Can I use that cart?

  A Yes, help yourself.

2 A Can you give me a hand?

  B What are you trying to do?

  A Take these books upstairs.

  B Sorry, but I have a bad back.

  A That's OK. Thanks anyway.

3 A Can you tell me the password?

  B I'm afraid I can't. I can't remember it.

  A Oh, come on.

  B No, really I can't. It's secret.

  A OK, it doesn't matter.

4 A Can I borrow your car tomorrow morning?

  B I'm sorry, but you're not insured.

  A Can you give me a lift to work, then?

  B OK. No problem.

5 A Can you hold the torch?

  B Yes.

  A And can you hold these nuts?

  B Yes.

  A And can you hold these bolts?

  B Yes.

A And can you pass me the screwdriver?
B I only have two hands, you know.

16.2

A Can you help me clean the CVS machine?
B Yes, but not today.
A Why not? Are you going out?
B No, but we have an order for 3,000 pieces.
A So we need the machine working?
B Yes, it only makes 500 pieces an hour.
A How long does it take to clean? An hour?
B No, it takes an hour to change the tools. Cleaning takes three hours.
A OK, let's do it tomorrow then.

16.3

A Gilles Prost.
B …
A Hello, Louisa. How are you?
B …
A Fine, thanks. What can I do for you, Louisa?
B …
A How much do you need?
B …
A So that's two bottles of alcohol. Anything else?
B …
A How many do you need?
B …
A So that's fifteen bandages. Anything else?
B …
A OK, I'll send them right away.
B …
A You're welcome.
B …
A Goodbye.

16.4

A Gilles Prost.
B Hello, Gilles. This is Louisa.
A Hello, Louisa. How are you?
B I'm fine, thanks. And you?
A Fine, thanks. What can I do for you, Louisa?
B We need some alcohol.
A How much do you need?
B Two bottles.
A So that's two bottles of alcohol. Anything else?

B Yes, I need some bandages.
A How many do you need?
B Fifteen.
A So that's fifteen bandages. Anything else?
B No, that's all, thanks.
A OK, I'll send them right away.
B Thanks very much.
A You're welcome.
B Goodbye.
A Goodbye.

16.5

1 3 multiplied by n equals 12
2 13 minus n equals 6
3 54 divided by n equals 6
4 3 plus 8 equals n
5 n multiplied by 3 equals 39
6 42 divided by n equals 7
7 14 minus 3 plus 2 equals n

17.1

1 A A ticket to Oxford, please.
   B Single or return?
   A Single.
   B That's £30.50 (thirty pounds fifty).
   A Which platform is it?
   B Platform nine.
   A Thanks.

2 A Do you have a visa for the United States?
   B No.
   A Then you need this green form for immigration.
   B Do you have one in Italian?
   A Sorry, no. But the flight magazine has instructions. Ask me for help if you need it.
   B And what's this white form?
   A It's for customs. You need to fill out both sides.

3 A Is this the Excel exhibition centre?
   B Yes, this is it.
   A Great. How much is that?
   B Thirteen pounds forty.
   A OK, can I have a receipt? Make it for sixteen dollars … I mean pounds.
   B Thanks very much.

4 A Is there just the one bag?
   B Yes.

A Does it contain any electrical items?
B Yes, a hairdryer.
A Has anyone given you anything to carry?
B No.
A Did you pack your bag yourself?
B Yes.
A Has it been in your possession at all times?
B Yes.

5 A What do you want to drink?
B No, let me get this.
A No, no, you can get the next one.
B OK. A pint of lager, please.
A What kind do you want? They have Kronenbourg, Heineken, …
B Kronenbourg is fine.

18.1

OK, this is what happens. The burning paper heats the air inside the bottle. The air expands and rises and some air gets out past the egg. The burning paper consumes all the oxygen inside the bottle and the fire goes out. Then the air inside the bottle cools down and contracts. That lowers the air pressure inside the bottle. And that means the air pressure outside the bottle is higher than the air pressure inside the bottle. That's why the egg falls into the bottle.

19.1

A This computer needs checking.
B I did some work on it this morning and I deleted a lot of old files.
A Oh, good. Did you use the checklist?
B No, sorry. I didn't.
A Then it needs filling in, but we can do it now. Did you empty the Recycle Bin?
B Yes, and I checked the hard drive for errors and it was OK.
A Did you run 'Defrag' and 'Cleanup'?
B Yes, I did. I downloaded a new service pack too.
A Did you update the drivers?
B Er, no. I didn't have time.
A OK, that still needs doing then. And did you do a back-up?
B Yes.

A Good. It isn't very clean, is it?
B But I cleaned everything.
A What about the keyboard?
B It's just old.
A Hmm. I think it needs cleaning again.

19.2

A Tom Parks.
B Hi, Tom, Chas here.
A Hi, Chas. What's up?
B It's the pump.
A What's wrong with it?
B It's leaking again.
A Did you check the hoses?
B Yes, they're all OK.
A What happens if you switch it off?
B It keeps on leaking.
A Do you want me to send an engineer?
B Yes, please. How soon can they be here?
A Five minutes. I'll send someone right away.
B Great. Thanks a lot.
A You're welcome.
B Bye.

20.1

1 Where are your goggles? You must put them on right away. This can hurt your eyes.
2 Don't lick your fingers and don't drink it. It's poisonous.
3 Can you smell it? It's *very* bad for you. You have to open all the windows and doors when you use it.
4 This box must *not* get wet. Keep it away from water.
5 Never light matches or cigarettes near this. Never put it near a flame.
6 Make sure the lid is very secure. Don't leave it half open.
7 Don't leave this bottle in a hot room. OK? Keep it in a cool place.
8 Do any children come in here? Don't allow them to touch this box.

20.2

A Hey, what's up?
B I had an accident.
A What happened?

B I tripped and cut my leg.
A Do you need a doctor?
B No, just a bandage. It's not a big cut.
A Will you be OK?
B Yes, I'll be fine.
A Why did you trip?
B There were some metal pipes on the floor.
   I didn't see them.
A Who left them there?
B I put them there yesterday and forgot
   about them.
A Ah! Don't leave things on the floor.
B I know. I won't do it again.

20.3

1 One hundred miles per hour is nought
   point oh four four seven kilometres per
   second.
2 One tonne is two thousand two hundred
   and five pounds.
3 One yard is nine hundred and fourteen
   point four millimetres.
4 One square metre is one thousand five
   hundred and fifty square inches.
5 One cubic foot is six point two two nine
   gallons.
6 One pound per square inch is zero
   point zero seven zero three one kilograms
   per square metre.
7 One hundred kilojoules is nought point oh
   two seven eight kilowatt hours.
8 Nought degrees Fahrenheit is minus
   seventeen point seven eight degrees Celsius.

21.1

The boom is the steel arm of the crane. It
runs up from behind the operator's cab and it
lifts the load. The hydraulic ram raises and
lowers the boom. It's a piston cylinder and it
pushes the boom up by pumping oil.

Just behind the operator's cab, there's a
winch. Cable lines run from the winch, up
and along the boom. They're attached to a
hook, and the hook carries the load.

There's a gear under the operator's cab. It
rotates the boom left and right. There are
outriggers attached to the sides of the truck.
They support the crane so that strong winds
can't blow it over.

21.2

A So, Lyle, tell me about these inventions.
   What's this one?
B It's a coat-hanger.
A Really?
B Yes, it's made of very thin latex and it's
   filled with helium gas.
A So it floats?
B Yes.
A And it's for hanging your shirts on the
   ceiling?
B That's right.
A Oh, very clever. What about this one?
B Oh, I need this device. I often put on odd
   socks.
A Show me ... Oh, yes. You're wearing one
   green sock and one brown sock.
B Am I? Oh!
A So this device is for checking your socks
   match?
B That's right.
A OK, next one. This is for painting walls,
   right?
B Yes, I hate painting walls. It takes too
   long, but this paintbrush is automatic. It
   saves time.
A Wonderful! What's this one? Is it a watch?
B Yes, but it has a map. I don't like
   shopping. This device is for finding my
   wife in a shopping mall.
A Oh, very useful. I think I can see your wife
   in this picture.
B Yes, that's Ann.
A And what's this device for?
B It's for saving gasoline. You attach the big
   magnet to a truck ...
A ...and it pulls you along?
B Yes, it's environmentally friendly.
A Lyle, it's fantastic!
B Oh, well, thank you very much. I love
   inventing machines.

UNIVERSITY PRESS

Great Clarendon Street, Oxford OX2 6DP

Oxford University Press is a department of the University of Oxford. It furthers the University's objective of excellence in research, scholarship, and education by publishing worldwide in

Oxford New York

Auckland Bangkok Buenos Aires Cape Town Chennai Dar es Salaam Delhi Hong Kong Istanbul Karachi Kolkata Kuala Lumpur Madrid Melbourne Mexico City Mumbai Nairobi São Paulo Shanghai Taipei Tokyo Toronto

Oxford and Oxford English are registered trade marks of Oxford University Press in the UK and in certain other countries

ISBN 0 19 457453 9

Printed in China

Acknowledgements

The author would like to thank her family, friends, and editors for their tolerance, expertise, and good humour during the writing of this manuscript. She'd also like to thank Rob Gibson, Andy Hewitson, and James Schofield at Siemens AG for helping to formulate the ideas for this book, along with John Sydes and Rob Hilliard at Target in Munich, and all the kind and knowledgeable teachers she met during her research. Merci beaucoup. And last but not least, a huge thank you to the wonderful technicians, scientists, and engineers at MTU for being the best guinea pigs an author could have. It was such fun!

The author and publisher would like to thank the following for their advice and assistance in the development of this course: Brian Cross, Phillipa Dralet, Judith Fearon, Rob Gibson, Anna Gunn, Phyllis Hâxell, Moira Jansen, Sally Jones, Paul Keogh, Pat Nickel, John Sydes, and Peggy Wegler.

Special thanks are also due to Matthew Gilbert, Rosemary Morlin, Shireen Nathoo, Helen Reilly, and Maki Ryan.

Illustrations by

Francis Blake/Three-in-a-box pp18, 29 (cubism), 39, 47 (coin), 49 (cartoons), 51, 52 (parking), 56 (bag), 61 (rocket), 81, 84, 90, 97 (window-closing machine), 107 (cartoon), 108 (bulb), 111 (cartoon), 114; Mark Duffin pp11, 14 (all), 15, 17, 20, 21, 28 (bottle), 37 (equipment), 41 (circuit board), 48 (bulbs), 50 (equipment), 54, 55, 56 (storeroom), 57 (water), 59, 62, 64, 65, 77, 82 (wheel), 85, 92, 93 (bottom), 102, 104, 115; Tim Kahane pp5 (rocket), 7 (karate), 13, 16, 24, 31, 45 (adjectives), 48 (this/that), 49 (trucks), 50 (adjectives), 63, 74, 75, 78 (hill), 88, 96 (crane), 101, 108 (car); Ben Kirchner/HEART pp6, 7 (robot), 46, 57 (room), 66, 78 (directions), 79, 89, 107 (room), 112, 113; SNDesign pp5 (all numbers), 8 (icons), 22, 23, 29 (optical illusions, simple shapes), 33 (Asimo movements), 37 (flags), 41 (wiring), 47 (all clocks), 48-49 (keys), 56 (keys), 78 (prepositions), 97 (top), 100, 105, 108 (wiring); Willie Ryan/Illustration Ltd pp7 (chair, window), 40, 45 (directions), 52 (signs – bottom), 80, 82 (5 diagrams), 91, 93, 103, 106 (spark plug); Harry Venning pp42-43, 53, 58, 78 (cartoons), 94.

The publisher would like to thank the following for their permission to reproduce photographs and other copyright material:

AAPhotolibrary p53; ABB p34 (IRB840); Alamy/The Motoring Picture Library p38 (car); Dino Brondolo p68 (Dino Brondolo); Corbis p71 (Chinese city); Dan McCormack (www.photographytips.com) p27 (carousel truck); Frank Didik p27 (Duplex scooter); Elekit Japan Co. Ltd p35 (Line Tracker and Hyper Peppy), 106; Foodpix/Getty Images p12 (cola); Friendly Robotics p34 (RL800); Fujifilm p101 (FinePix 603 Zoom camera); Fraunhofer-Gesellschaft p34 (Sirius); GM Media Archive p26; Hewlett Packard p101 (printer); Image Bank/Getty Images p101 (gloves); Image State/Stuart Pearce p36; Kerry McClean p27 (monowheel); Maarit Lehtinen p27 (kick sled); Lynxmotion (www.lynxmotion.com) p35 (Hexapod Walker); NASA p34 Canada Arm, 68 (ISS), 69 and 111(Roger Curbeam), 95; NASDA p69 and p111 (Takayoshi Nishikawa); Panos p71 and 110 (boy/water); Photodisc (OUP Assets) pp12 (hamburger, cheeseburger, hotdog, sandwich, doughnut, milkshake), 38 (train, balloon, plane); Photodisc p12 fries, 28 (shoes), 70, 81 (X-ray); QA Photos p67; Rex Features p27 (funfair bike, quadrant bike/car), 34 (Robug); Smarthome p82 (car jack), 101 (insect trap); Stone/Getty Images p71 (Hindu worship), 110; Monster Robots Inc p35 (Robosaurus); Panther p101 (air compressor); Rex Features Ltd p71 (grandad), 110; Sony p32 (Asimo), 34 (Aibo); Science Photo Library p25 (all), 33 (body parts); Sylvie Beland p69; Taxi/Getty Images p9; The Motoring Picture Library p27 (Land Rover); Thinkstock/Getty Images p27 (stretch limo); Vortech p39 (Skylark); WHMTool Group p93 (the safety instructions are for the purpose of this exercise only and are not to be followed).

The author and publisher would like to thank the following for their permission to reproduce copyright cartoons: Lyle B Clarke p98; Rube Goldberg Inc (Rube Goldberg is the ® and © of Rube Goldberg Inc) p96.

Studio and location photography by

Emily Andersen p4; Steve Betts pp60 (survival kit), 76 (medical kit); SNDesign pp10, 12 (coffee), 28, 33 (items), 74, 77, 88 (computer).

Although every effort has been made to contact copyright holders before publication, in some cases this has not been possible. We apologize for any apparent infringement of copyright and, if contacted, the publisher will be pleased to rectify any errors or omissions at the earliest opportunity.